Bravo ASL! Curriculum

Student Workbook

Jenna Deborah Cassell

and

Dr. Len Roberson

ISBN 1-882872-97-5

American Sign Language Productions, Inc.
Jenna Cassell, President and Founder
San Diego, CA 92109

1-800-767-4461
www.signenhancers.com

Dedication

To all students of American Sign Language
whose hearts aspire to use their hands to speak their minds.

The Beginning ASL VideoCourse (affectionately known as "the Bravo family tapes") is the recipient of the following awards: Silver Telly Award (1993), Parents' Choice Honor (1994), Kid's First Honor (1995), International CINDY Award (1996), Bronze Telly (2007), and two Communicator Awards (2008).

Welcome to Bravo ASL!
The Beginning American Sign Language Course

This comprehensive first-year American Sign Language course is designed to provide you with one successful learning experience after another, making it fun to build your language skills as you gain an understanding of the culture of Deaf people. Regardless of what your reasons are for wanting to learn ASL, or your personal learning style, *Bravo ASL!* provides the support you need to succeed.

This Student Workbook and the companion 15-DVD *Beginning American Sign Language VideoCourse* feature Instructor Billy Seago and the Bravo family guiding you through the lessons as they share their daily life experiences. As you watch this fun-loving family (including two Deaf children, a Deaf father and a hearing mother), you will learn new language skills that you'll be able to immediately apply within the context of signed communication!

This workbook will be your personal record of your American Sign Language progress and a place to jot down notes, questions, and ideas for class projects. It is designed to help you get the most from this course.

What's included in your Student Workbook?

Lesson Objectives: The objectives tell you what to expect to learn in each lesson.

Activity Goals and Instructions: The goals and the instructions for each activity are clearly explained to help you accomplish the lesson's objectives.

Visual Aids and Worksheets: Pictures, worksheets, puzzles, and a variety of written materials make it enjoyable to participate in each of the lesson's activities.

Content Outlines: Don't worry about taking too many notes. This workbook provides outlines of all the main points contained in the signed presentations about culture and grammar.

Quizzes: Do you want to know how you are doing? Quizzes check your ASL comprehension skills and your understanding of the cultural and grammatical information.

Thought/Discussion Questions: To help you get the most from classroom activities, Thought/Discussion Questions are provided. You will address these questions in class or your instructor will ask you to do them independently.

Homework Assignments: Out-of-class assignments give you an opportunity to strengthen your skills and deepen your understanding of the course materials.

Sign Illustration Section: Illustrations of the ASL sign vocabulary can be found in the Sign Illustration Section at the end of this Workbook. This section is organized according to lesson number and indexed alphabetically for easy access. Use these illustrations to help you to remember how to accurately produce each sign.

Congratulations on choosing to learn American Sign Language! This *Bravo ASL!* course will make learning this beautiful language fun and rewarding. We put Sign Language communication within reach... now it's in your hands!

Note: In recognition and respect of the culture of Deaf people, the word Deaf is capitalized throughout all written materials associated with this course.

Lesson 1
MEET THE BRAVO FAMILY

1.2 Pretest

What Do You Know?

Pretest Goal: To see how much you already know about what will be taught in this lesson.

Pretest Instructions: Read and answer each question.

1. Deaf people actually have their own culture.
   A. True
   B. False

2. American Sign Language is not a real language, it is a shortened form of English.
   A. True
   B. False

3. In ASL, a statement can become a question by simply raising the eyebrows and tilting the head slightly.
   A. True
   B. False

4. The sign for LOVE looks like you are hugging someone.
   A. True
   B. False

5. If you want to get a Deaf person's attention, it would be appropriate to flash the lights.
   A. True
   B. False

6. If you want to get a Deaf person's attention, it would be appropriate to throw a light object at him/her.
   A. True
   B. False

7. ASL grammar is the same as English grammar except that ASL is visual.
   A. True
   B. False

1.3 Lesson Objectives

Planning for Success

Goal: To see what you will learn by the end of this lesson.

Instructions: Read the objectives below.

Upon completing this VideoCourse lesson, you will be able to...

1. Identify the four members of the Bravo family (including their names, name signs, who is Deaf, who is hearing and the children's ages).

2. Recognize and accurately produce the ASL vocabulary introduced in this lesson.

3. Identify Deaf people as a cultural group with their own language, customs and values.

4. Describe culturally appropriate ways to get a Deaf person's attention.

5. Describe culturally appropriate ways to wake a Deaf person.

6. Identify ASL as a distinct language with its own grammatical rules.

7. Recognize and identify yes/no and wh-question types.

8. Accurately produce yes/no and wh-question types including the non-manual grammatical markers associated with each.

1.4 Lesson Focus

Meet The Fam

Activity Goal: To introduce yourself and your family to classmates without using your voice.

Activity Instructions: Take turns introducing yourself to your classmates. Share information about your family, such as if there is a mother, father, daughter, son, etc.

Remember, do not use your voice! You may use signs, gestures, fingerspelling, mime (acting things out), pointing, etc. Be creative, and have fun!

PS: Don't worry, after this lesson, you will have the sign vocabulary you need to introduce your family.

Thought/Discussion Questions

1. What are some signs related to family introductions that would have been useful to know during this activity?

   _____

   _____

   _____

2. How did it feel to be limited in your ability to communicate?

   _____

   _____

   _____

3. What are some ways that Deaf people could introduce their families to people who don't sign?

   _____

   _____

   _____

1.5 Video Learning Experience

LESSON ONE

Meet the Bravo Family

Viewing Goal: To identify the members of the Bravo family including their names, who is Deaf and who is hearing, and the children's ages.

Viewing Instructions: After viewing the introduction of Billy and the Bravo family, fill in the Bravo family tree below.

The Bravo Family Tree

The Bravo Dad

Name: _____
__ Deaf __ Hearing

The Bravo Mom

Name: _____
__ Deaf __ Hearing

The Bravo Daughter

Name: _____
__ Deaf __ Hearing
Age: ____

The Bravo Son

Name: _____
__ Deaf __ Hearing
Age: ____

1.6 Language Learning Instruction

Learning New Signs

Goal: To help you learn new ASL vocabulary.

Instructions: Your instructor will teach you new signs! Watch closely to learn what these signs mean and how they are produced.

In the space below, record any notes to help you remember the signs.

_____

_____

_____

_____

_____

_____

_____

_____

_____

_____

1.7 Video Learning Experience

Introduction to New Vocabulary

Viewing Goal: To help you learn new ASL vocabulary.

Viewing Instructions: Watch how Billy produces each sign. Be sure to notice the facial/body expressions. Copy the signs as Billy repeats each one.

Signs representing the following concepts are introduced in this video segment:

1. MOM/MOTHER
2. CHILDREN
3. BABY
4. GOOD
5. MORNING
6. COFFEE
7. HUNGRY
8. YES
9. NO
10. THANK-YOU
11. WHERE
12. LOVE
13. DEAF
14. HEARING
15. WHICH
16. WANT
17. TOILET/BATHROOM
18. BRUSH-TEETH
19. TIME
20. WAKE-UP
21. SCHOOL
22. BREAKFAST
23. PAST/BEFORE
24. GO

_____

_____

_____

_____

_____

_____

_____

_____

Note: Illustrations of each ASL sign can be found in the Sign Illustration Section at the back of this Student Workbook.

1.8 Experiential Activity

Point and Sign

Activity Goal: To help you recognize the new ASL vocabulary within the context of signed communication.

Activity Instructions: Your instructor will point to some pictures and ask you questions using ASL. Watch carefully and follow your instructor's directions in responding to these questions.

1.9 Video Learning Experience

Bravo Family Visit

Viewing Goal: To improve your ASL comprehension skills by watching a Bravo family interaction.

Viewing Instructions: Watch the signed interaction and write a summary of the main points (in your own words) to help you remember.

_____

_____

_____

_____

_____

_____

_____

_____

1.10 Comprehension Quiz

What Did You Understand?

Quiz Goal: To see how much of the Bravo family interaction you understood.

Quiz Instructions: Read and answer each question below.

1. Dad offers Mom coffee. Does she want any?
   A. Yes
   B. No

2. Mom asks Dad where the children are. What does he tell her?
   A. "At school."
   B. "Eating breakfast."
   C. "Sleeping upstairs."
   D. "Playing with the dog."

3. What does Anna ask Mom?
   A. "A long time ago, did you want a hearing or Deaf baby?"
   B. "A long time ago, did you have a hearing baby?"
   C. "Did you want all your babies to be Deaf?"
   D. "Did you want all your babies to be hearing?"

4. How does Mom answer this question?
   A. "I want you to shower."
   B. "I wanted a hearing child."
   C. "I wanted a Deaf child."
   D. "I wanted you."

5. When Mom asks Anna if she wanted a Deaf or hearing mom, Anna said she would have preferred a Deaf mom, but she loves her mom anyway.
   A. True
   B. False

1.11 Experiential Activity

Point and Sign

Activity Goal: To help you recognize and produce the new ASL vocabulary.

Activity Instructions: Using the pictures below, follow your teacher's instructions and practice using your new sign vocabulary such as: MOTHER, FATHER, BABY, LOVE, WHERE, DEAF, HEARING, HUNGRY, CHILDREN, BATHROOM, WHICH, YES, NO and GOOD.

1.12 Language Learning Instruction

Learning New Signs

Goal: To help you learn new ASL vocabulary.

Instructions: Your instructor will teach you new signs! Watch closely to learn what these signs mean and how they are produced.

In the space below, record any notes to help you remember the signs.

_____

_____

_____

_____

_____

_____

_____

Note: Remember, you can find illustrations of each sign in the Illustration Section at the end of this workbook.

1.13 Video Learning Experience

LESSON ONE

Introduction to New Vocabulary

Viewing Goal: To help you learn new ASL vocabulary.

Viewing Instructions: Watch how Billy produces each sign. Be sure to notice the facial/body expressions. Copy the signs as Billy repeats each one.

Signs representing the following concepts are introduced in this video segment:

1. DOG
2. FOOL-YOU
3. SHOWER
4. KITCHEN (COOK+ROOM)
5. SON (BOY+BABY)
6. DAUGHTER (GIRL+BABY)
7. SCARED/AFRAID
8. BED
9. SPIDER
10. ALMOST
11. GET-DRESSED

1.14 Experiential Activity

Point and Sign

Activity Goal: To help you recognize the new ASL vocabulary within the context of signed communication.

Activity Instructions: Your instructor will point to some pictures and ask you questions using ASL. Watch carefully and follow your instructor's directions in responding to these questions.

1.15 Video Learning Experience

LESSON ONE

Bravo Family Visit

Viewing Goal: To improve ASL comprehension skills by watching a Bravo family interaction.

Viewing Instructions: Watch the signed interaction and write a summary of the main points (in your own words) to help you remember.

_____

_____

_____

_____

_____

_____

_____

_____

1.16 Comprehension Quiz

What Did You Understand?

Quiz Goal: To see how much of the Bravo family interaction you understood.

Quiz Instructions: Read and answer each question below.

---

1. When Mom went into Scott's room, what did she find in his bed?

   A. There was a spider on Scott's head.
   B. A spider was in the dog's mouth.
   C. The dog was in the bed with Scott.
   D. The dog was in bed instead of Scott.

2. Did Scott fool Mom?

   A. Yes, she almost sent the dog to school.
   B. No, she knew the spider was there the whole time.
   C. No, she knew the dog was there the whole time.
   D. Yes, she thought the spider was the dog.

3. How does Mom feel about spiders?

   A. She eats them for breakfast.
   B. She is scared of them.
   C. She likes them better than dogs.
   D. She didn't want to talk about it because it was time for breakfast.

4. Scott wanted to go straight to school since he was not very hungry.

   A. True
   B. False

1.17 Video Learning Experience

Handwritten notes in left margin:
Tests of Lesson
Multiple Choice of Short Answer
2. Culture of Granny
3. Expression
Section

Cultural Notes

Viewing Goal: To learn about the cultural aspects of ASL.

Viewing Instructions: View the *Cultural Notes* segment carefully for the following:

I. Deaf people have their own distinct culture:

    A. Deaf Culture is equal to that of other cultures such as American, French, or English cultures.

    B. Just like all cultures, Deaf culture includes a set of shared customs and values.

    C. As in any language instruction, cultural information must be included when learning ASL.

II. Culturally appropriate ways to get a Deaf person's attention include:

    A. A gentle tap on the shoulder.

    B. Waving one's hand toward the Deaf person.

    C. Calling out in a low tone.

    D. Stomping a foot that causes a vibration.

III. To wake a Deaf person it would be appropriate to use:

    A. A brief flashing of the light.

    B. A gentle tap.

1.18 Experiential Activity

Hey, You...

Activity Goal: To apply culturally appropriate ways of getting a Deaf person's attention.

Activity Instructions: Your instructor will divide the class into small groups. Within your group, take turns role-playing a Deaf person in each of the situations below while the other group members try to get his/her attention.

You want to get your Deaf friend's attention but s/he is...

1. Looking in the other direction.
2. Standing in line, two people ahead of you.
3. Chatting in ASL with some other Deaf friends.
4. Sitting down, reading a book.
5. Working on a computer.
6. Sleeping.

Thought/Discussion Questions

1. How did it feel to be the Deaf person? Were there any attempts to get your attention you felt were rude or not effective?

_____

_____

_____

2. When you were trying to get the Deaf person's attention, what worked the best?

_____

_____

_____

3. Did you try any new techniques not described by the video? What were the results?

_____

_____

_____

Note: Remember that although it is helpful to role-play within the educational setting, it is not appropriate to act Deaf outside the learning environment.

1.19 Video Learning Experience

LESSON ONE

Grammatical Notes

Viewing Goal: To learn about the grammatical aspects of ASL.

Viewing Instructions: View the *Grammatical Notes* segment carefully for the following:

I. ASL grammar and English grammar are different.

II. There are many ways of asking questions in ASL. This lesson focuses on two:

A. The yes/no question format elicits a YES or NO response. The non-manual grammatical markers associated with a yes/no question are:
   1. The eyebrows are raised.
   2. The head is slightly tilted.
   3. The eyes make direct contact.
   4. The last sign is held, waiting for a response.

B. The wh-question format asks who, what, where, when, how, which, why, etc. The non-manual grammatical markers associated with a wh-question are:
   1. The eyebrows are furrowed (down).
   2. The head is slightly tilted.
   3. The last sign is held, waiting for a response.

Note: As you can see above, the term "non-manual grammatical marker" refers to physical movements (other than the actual signs) including eyebrow raise/furrow, eye gaze, head tilt, mouth movements, and others. These markers provide important grammatical information such as question types.

1.20 Experiential Activity

What Kind of Question is That?!

Activity Goal: To apply the grammatical information you learned.

Activity Instructions: You will see several signed questions. Watch each sample closely and decide whether the question is a yes/no or a wh-question.

Don't worry if you do not understand the meaning of the sentence, just watch the non-manual grammatical markers to determine your answer.

Circle your answer:

1. yes/no   wh   6. yes/no   wh
2. yes/no   wh   7. yes/no   wh
3. yes/no   wh   8. yes/no   wh
4. yes/no   wh   9. yes/no   wh
5. yes/no   wh   10. yes/no   wh

1.21 Experiential Activity

Pass the Question

Activity Goal: To recognize and produce the non-manual grammatical markers for ASL question types within the context of a game.

Activity Instructions: This game is similar to "The Rumor Game." Your instructor will divide your class into teams. Each team will line up, single file, facing away from the teacher.

Your instructor will show the first student in each line a signed question. That student will watch carefully, tap the next student in line and repeat the question (including the non-manual grammatical markers). Each team will continue to pass the question until the last student in the line sees it.

The last student in each line must sign the question. If correct, this student goes to the board and writes whether it is a yes/no or a wh-question. If not correct, the team begins again with the first student passing the question to the second person in line, and so on.

The first team to demonstrate the correct question (including the non-manual markers) and write the correct question type on the board wins.

Good luck and have fun!

1.22
Cultural and
Grammatical
Quiz

What Did You Learn?

Quiz Goal: To see how much of this lesson's cultural and grammatical information you learned.

Quiz Instructions: Read and answer each question below.

1. Deaf people do not have their own culture because they belong to the American culture.
   A. True
   B. False ⟵

2. Cultural information must be included within any language learning experience.
   A. True ⟵
   B. False

3. The French, German and American people have distinct cultures, but Deaf people only belong to a community.
   A. True
   B. False ⟵

4. All cultures, including that of Deaf people, include customs and values.
   A. True ⟵
   B. False

5. Culturally appropriate ways for getting a Deaf person's attention include (check all that apply):
   ✗ A gentle tap on the shoulder
   ✗ Wave one's hand toward the Deaf person
   ✗ Call out in a low tone
   ✗ Stomp a foot causing a vibration
   __ Gently spray water at the Deaf person

6. Culturally appropriate ways for waking a Deaf person include (check all that apply):
   ✗ A light flashed briefly
   ✗ A gentle tap
   __ Gently spray water at the Deaf person

7. The non-manual markers associated with a <u>yes/no</u> question are (check all that apply):
   __ Eyebrows raised   ___ Slight head tilt
   __ Eyebrows furrowed   ___ Lean back
   ✗ Direct eye contact   ___ Last sign held for response

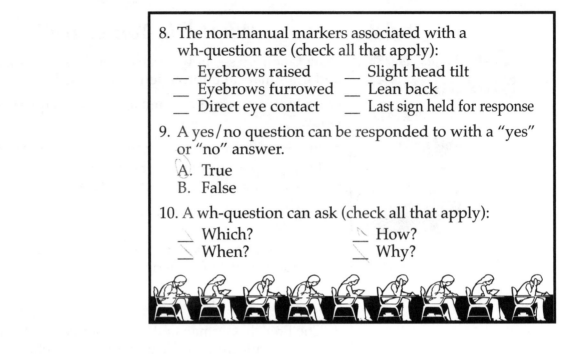

8. The non-manual markers associated with a wh-question are (check all that apply):
   __ Eyebrows raised   __ Slight head tilt
   __ Eyebrows furrowed   __ Lean back
   __ Direct eye contact   __ Last sign held for response

9. A yes/no question can be responded to with a "yes" or "no" answer.
   A. True
   B. False

10. A wh-question can ask (check all that apply):
   __ Which?   __ How?
   __ When?   __ Why?

1.23 Video Learning Experience

LESSON ONE

Review Session

Viewing Goal: To help you remember how to produce the signs introduced in this lesson.

Viewing Instructions: Watch this video segment carefully to see how each sign is made, and take note of any hints given that might help you remember. You may want to copy the signs as you watch Billy.

The following are the vocabulary and explanations offered in this video segment:

MORNING	One arm becomes the horizon. The other hand is the sun rising.
GOOD	This sign is a symbol representing the concept GOOD.
COFFEE	This sign comes from the old hand-operated coffee grinder.
NO	N-O, this was originally spelled out. This has since evolved into a sign.
THANK-YOU	This sign is like blowing a kiss.
HUNGRY	This sign shows there's no food in your stomach. You're empty.
CHILDREN	This sign is as if you are patting children on the head.
WHERE	This is a symbol representing the concept WHERE.

TIME	This sign refers to a watch on the wrist.
WAKE-UP	You're sleeping and when you wake up, your eyes open.
NOW	The space in front of the body represents the future. The space behind the body is the past. Directly in front and close to the body is NOW.
PAST	Remember the space behind the body represents the PAST.
OK	This sign is spelled out... O-K.
MOTHER	In ASL, feminine signs tend to occur on or near the chin.
GIRL	This sign comes from the bonnets worn long ago and represents the strap tied under the chin.
FATHER	ASL tends to place masculine signs on or near the forehead.
BOY	This sign comes from the brim of a baseball cap.
BABY	This looks like holding a baby.
DAUGHTER	A compound sign combining the signs for GIRL and BABY.
SON	Another compound sign using the signs BOY and BABY.
YES	This sign represents the head nodding YES.
WHAT	This is a symbol representing the concept of WHAT.
HEARING	This sign really means people who can talk. But, I want to make it clear that this doesn't mean Deaf people cannot talk. It means that Deaf people cannot hear themselves talk.
DEAF	This means that the ears and the mouth are closed. Again, this does not mean Deaf people can't talk, because most
WANT	There are things out there that you want, so you pull them to you.
WHICH	On one side is "yes," on the other side is "no"... WHICH will it be?
LOVE	This sign shows holding the one you love close to your heart.
BRUSH-TEETH	This looks like brushing your teeth.
GET-DRESSED	This sign shows the activity of putting clothes on.
SCHOOL	When teachers want a class's attention, they clap their hands.
READY	This sign shows your body poised and ready to go, using the "R" handshapes.
BATHROOM/TOILET	This is the symbol for BATHROOM. The "T" represents the "T" in TOILET.
GO	You're in one place and you want to go to another place. This sign represents that movement.

LESSON ONE

DOG	When you want a dog's attention, you whistle or slap your thighs.
MY/MINE	These signs show possession: MINE, OURS, HIS, and HERS.
FOOL-YOU	The index finger on one hand represents a person and the other hand is hitting (fooling) that person.
ALMOST	One hand slides up the other hand, not all the way to the top, but ALMOST.
SHOWER	This sign represents the water spraying down on you.
BREAKFAST	This is a compound sign combining FOOD and MORNING.
KITCHEN	This is another compound sign combining the signs for COOK and ROOM.

1.24 Video Learning Experience

Practice Session: Sentences

Viewing Goal: To improve your comprehension skills by watching sentences presented in ASL.

Viewing Instructions: Watch the signed sentences for comprehension. Remember to watch the face of each signer to see the facial/body expressions and the non-manual grammatical markers as well as the signs.

It is recommended that you copy each signed sentence when it is repeated.

In the space below, record any questions or notes you have regarding the sentences.

_____

_____

_____

_____

_____

_____

_____

_____

_____

_____

1.25 Experiential Activity

What's the Sentence About?

Activity Goal: To improve your comprehension skills using sentences presented in ASL.

Activity Instructions: You will see five signed sentences. Each sentence will be signed twice. Determine what each sentence is about and circle the correct answer below:

1. A. Going to school
   B. A morning greeting
   C. Taking a shower

2. A. Looking for Dad
   B. Looking for Daughter
   C. Looking for Mom

3. A. Needing a bathroom
   B. Needing a drink
   C. Needing a shower

4. A. Time to eat
   B. Time to brush your teeth
   C. Time to have coffee

5. A. Asking about school
   B. Asking about work
   C. Asking about breakfast

1.26
Experiential
Activity

It's Just a Drill!

Activity Goal: To improve your expressive skills by doing practice drills.

Activity Instructions: With a partner, practice the following drills together. Remember to include the non-manual question markers to identify the type of question you are asking.

COFFEE, $\overline{\text{WANT}}^{\text{q}}$
SHOWER,
GO SCHOOL,

MOTHER, $\overline{\text{WHERE}}^{\text{wh-q}}$
FATHER,
SON,
DAUGHTER,

HUNGRY, $\overline{\text{YOU}}^{\text{q}}$
MOTHER,
GO SCHOOL,
READY,

BATHROOM, $\overline{\text{YOU GO}}^{\text{q}}$
SCHOOL,
KITCHEN,

BRUSH-TEETH, $\overline{\text{YOU}}^{\text{q}}$
HEARING,
DEAF,
WAKE-UP,

Note: A "q" means this is a yes/no question. A "wh-q" means it is a wh-question type. To review how to produce these question types, see the *Grammatical Notes* (activity 1.19).

1.27 Video Learning Experience

Practice Session: Story

Viewing Goal: To improve your comprehension skills by watching a story presented in ASL.

Viewing Instructions: Watch the signed story for comprehension. In the space below, write a summary of the main points from the story.

_____

_____

_____

_____

_____

_____

_____

_____

_____

_____

1.28
Comprehension Quiz

What Did You Understand?

Quiz Goal: To see how much of the signed story you understood.

Quiz Instructions: Read and answer each question below.

1. When did this story take place?

   _____

2. Where did the story take place?

   _____

3. Who was there?

   _____

4. What did the children want?

   _____

   _____

5. What did Mom want the children to do?

   _____

   _____

6. How did the son respond?

   _____

   _____

7. How did the daughter respond?

   _____

   _____

8. What did the mother suggest?

   _____

   _____

9. Did the daughter want to do that?

   _____

   _____

10. What did the daughter decide to do?

    _____

    _____

LESSON ONE

1.29 Homework Assignment

Meet My Family

Homework Goal: To help you improve your ASL expressive skills.

Homework Instructions: For the next class session, bring in a picture(s) of your own family, or one pictured in a magazine. Be prepared to "introduce" each person in the picture(s) by pointing and using the new ASL vocabulary.

1.30 Post-test Introduction

What Do You Know Now?

Post-test Goal: To assess your mastery of the lesson objectives.

Post-test Introduction: This test has three sections.

Section One: The Comprehension section tests your ability to understand ASL.

Section Two: The Culture and Grammar section tests your knowledge of the material presented in the *Cultural* and *Grammatical Notes.*

Section Three: The Expressive Portion tests your ability to use ASL.

Simply follow the instructions for each section.

Good luck!

Lesson 2
BREAKFAST WITH THE BRAVO FAMILY

2.2 Homework Review

Meet My Family

Activity Goal: To show what you did for homework.

Activity Instructions: Take out the picture(s) of your own family or a family pictured in a magazine. Using ASL, introduce each person in the picture(s) by pointing and using the ASL vocabulary.

2.3 Pretest

What Do You Know?

Pretest Goal: To see how much you already know about what will be taught in this lesson.

Pretest Instructions: Read each question and circle the best answer.

1. Deaf people should be viewed with pity.
   A. True
   B. False

2. Families with Deaf members can be closely connected.
   A. True
   B. False

3. Like English, adjectives in ASL are usually placed before the noun.
   A. True
   B. False

4. Signs can be modified by changing the movement of the sign.
   A. True
   B. False

5. Adjectives can be modified simply by changing facial expressions.
   A. True
   B. False

2.4 Lesson Objectives

Planning for Success

Goal: To see what you will learn by the end of this lesson.

Instructions: Read the objectives below.

Upon completing this VideoCourse lesson, you will be able to...

1. Recognize and accurately produce the ASL vocabulary introduced in this and the previous lesson.

2. Describe two distinct perspectives generally held regarding members of the Deaf community.

3. Use noun/adjective combinations appropriately in ASL.

4. Demonstrate how signs can be modified in ASL.

2.5 Lesson Focus

That's NOT What I Ordered!

Activity Goal: To practice communicating about breakfast without using your voice.

Activity Instructions: Your instructor will divide the class into small groups. Each group will role-play going out to breakfast. Select one student to be the "server" while the other members are the "diners."

When ordering breakfast, all participants should use mime, gestures, or signs. The diners are not to write or use their voices.

The server should write down the order as s/he understood it. After all the orders in the group have been taken, see if the order taken was what you wanted. Enjoy your breakfast!

Thought/Discussion Questions

1. What are some signs related to ordering breakfast that would have been useful to know during this activity?

_____

_____

_____

_____

2. How did it feel to be limited in your ability to communicate?

_____

_____

_____

_____

3. When Deaf people go out to a restaurant, what are some communication techniques they could use?

_____

_____

_____

_____

2.6 Language Learning Instruction

Learning New Signs

Goal: To help you learn new ASL vocabulary.

Instructions: Your instructor will teach you new signs! Watch closely to learn what these signs mean and how they are produced.

In the space below, record any notes to help you remember the signs.

_____

_____

_____

_____

_____

_____

_____

_____

2.7 Video Learning Experience

Introduction to New Vocabulary

Viewing Goal: To help you learn the new ASL vocabulary.

Viewing Instructions: Watch how Billy produces each sign. Be sure to notice the facial/body expressions. Copy the signs as Billy repeats each one.

Signs representing the following concepts are introduced in this video segment:

1.	COOK	15.	SET+TABLE
2.	EAT	16.	PLATE
3.	EGG	17.	GLASS
4.	TOAST	18.	FORK
5.	CEREAL	19.	KNIFE
6.	ORANGE+JUICE	20.	SPOON
7.	BANANA	21.	NAPKIN
8.	MILK	22.	WORK
9.	ONE	23.	DO-WHAT
10.	TWO	24.	WASH
11.	GIVE	25.	HELP
12.	TELL	26.	MY-TURN
13.	WAITER	27.	YOUR-TURN
14.	GONE	28.	YESTERDAY

2.8 Experiential Activity

Point and Sign

Activity Goal: To help you recognize the new ASL vocabulary within the context of signed communication.

Activity Instructions: Your instructor will point to some pictures and ask you questions using ASL. Watch carefully and follow your instructor's directions in responding to these questions.

2.9 Video Learning Experience

Bravo Family Visit

Viewing Goal: To improve your ASL comprehension skills by watching a Bravo family interaction.

Viewing Instructions: Watch the signed interaction and write a summary of the main points.

_____

_____

_____

_____

_____

_____

_____

_____

2.10 Comprehension Quiz

What Did You Understand?

Quiz Goal: To see how much of the Bravo family interaction you understood.

Quiz Instructions: Read and answer each question below.

1. Mom wants a(n) _____ for breakfast.
   A. Orange
   B. Banana
   C. Piece of toast
   D. Bowl of cereal

2. Scott orders _____ egg(s)
   A. One
   B. Two
   C. Three
   D. Four

3. Scott also orders a _____ glass of orange juice.
  A. Small
  B. Large

4. Anna orders _____ to drink.
  A. Milk
  B. Water
  C. Orange juice
  D. Coffee

5. Who will be washing the dishes after breakfast?
  A. Mom
  B. Dad
  C. Anna
  D. Scott

2.11 Experiential Activity

Point and Sign

Activity Goal: To help you recognize and produce the new ASL vocabulary.

Activity Instructions: Using the picture below, follow your teacher's instructions and practice using your new ASL vocabulary such as: MILK, FATHER, SON, DAUGHTER, BANANA, ORANGE, COFFEE, PLATE, GLASS, EAT, COOK, WASH, SET+TABLE, etc.

2.12 Video Learning Experience

LESSON TWO

Cultural Notes

Viewing Goal: To learn about the cultural aspects of ASL.

Viewing Instructions: View the *Cultural Notes* segment carefully for the following:

I. Families with Deaf members can be very closely connected.

   A. The Bravo family is an example of how families with Deaf members can be warm and fun-loving.

   B. The Bravos demonstrate how wit and cleverness can be used for enhancing the enjoyment of life.

II. There are two common ways of looking at Deaf people:

   A. The handicapped perspective:

     1. This perspective views Deaf people with pity.

     2. This perspective emphasizes what Deaf people can't do...

       a. Can't hear.
       b. Can't talk.
       c. Can't laugh.
       d. Can't live a normal, full life.

     3. This perspective perceives being Deaf as a problem that needs to be fixed.

   B. The cultural perspective:

     1. This perspective views Deaf people as belonging to a culture equal with all the other cultures of the world.

     2. This perspective views Deaf people in a positive light, focusing on the potential of Deaf people...

       a. Deaf people can have full lives.
       b. They can laugh.
       c. They have sorrows.
       d. They have good times and bad.

III. Deaf people are equal to all other peoples.

IV. All people and all cultures should be respected.

V. The Deaf culture exists all around us, making it readily accessible to people wishing to enhance their cultural awareness.

2.13 Experiential Activity

A Cultural Adventure!

Activity Goal: To provide you with a new cultural experience!

Activity Instructions: Your class will be divided into two cultures: The Grokkers and the Artifs.

Each culture will live in a different room. When you join your group, you will receive a cultural orientation.

You will also have the opportunity to visit the other culture! Enjoy the experience!

Thought/Discussion Questions

1. How would you describe the other culture?

   A. What customs did you observe?

   _____

   B. What do you think was important to the members of this cultural group?

   _____

   _____

2. What was it like for you when you went to visit the other culture?

   A. How did you feel about the other culture?

   _____

   B. Did you feel welcome and comfortable?

   _____

   C. How did you communicate? Did you learn the language?

   _____

   D. What were you able to learn about their culture?

   _____

3. Do you think this is similar to how Deaf people feel in an environment that is dominated by the hearing culture and its values? Give some examples.

   _____

   _____

   _____

   _____

2.14 Video Learning Experience

Grammatical Notes

Viewing Goal: To learn about the grammatical aspects of ASL.

Viewing Instructions: View the *Grammatical Notes* segment carefully for the following:

I. Adjectives:
  A. The English language tends to place the adjective before the noun.
  B. ASL tends to put the adjective after the noun.

II. Adjectives can be modified by:
  A. Changing the movement of the sign.
  B. Using facial expressions.
  C. Using body language.

III. Signs can be modified by:
  A. Inflection.
  B. Repetition.
  C. Placement or location.

2.15 Experiential Activity

Modify Me!

Activity Goal: To use the grammatical information by modifying the meaning of various signs.

Activity Instructions: Practice signing the list of vocabulary words below. Using only the signs listed, practice modifying the production of these signs to show the various meanings shown next to each sign. Use inflection, repetition and changing the location as discussed in the *Grammatical Notes* segment.

Note: Remember to use the appropriate facial/body expressions!

Sign	Modify the sign to show...			
WORK	a short time	a long time	really hard	very easy
COOK	a short time	a long time	boring	fun
EAT	quickly	slowly	a long time	a lot of food
GIVE	a lot to you	a little to me	to everyone	over and over
TELL	many people	one person	a secret	over and over
HELP	many people	me quickly	struggling	over and over
WANT	desperately	excitedly	many things	begging
GO	many places	same place	happily	sadly

2.16 Culture and Grammar Quiz

What Did You Learn?

Quiz Goal: To see how much of this lesson's cultural and grammatical information you learned.

Quiz Instructions: Read and answer each question below.

1. Families with Deaf members can be closely connected.
   A. True
   B. False

2. The handicapped perspective views Deaf people in a positive manner.
   A. True
   B. False

3. The culture of Deaf people is equal to all other cultures.
   A. True
   B. False

4. The cultural perspective views Deaf people as having full lives.
   A. True
   B. False

5. Adjective placement in ASL follows the same rules as adjective placement in English.
   A. True
   B. False

6. In ASL, adjectives tend to be placed _____.
   A. Before the noun
   B. At the end of the sentence
   C. After the noun
   D. At the beginning of the sentence

7. Adjectives are modified in the following ways (check all that apply):
   __ Changing the movement of the sign
   __ Changing facial expression
   __ Changing body language
   __ Changing dominant/non-dominant hands

8. Signs can be modified by (check all that apply):
   __ Inflection of language
   __ Repetition
   __ Slight head tilt
   __ Changing location/placement

2.17 Video Learning Experience

Review Session

Viewing Goal: To help you remember how to produce the signs introduced in this lesson.

Viewing Instructions: Watch this video segment carefully to see how each sign is made, and take note of any hints given that might help you remember. You may want to copy the signs as you watch Billy.

The following are the vocabulary and explanations offered in this video segment:

EAT	Where does the food go? In your mouth.
EGG	This sign reflects breaking an eggshell.
TOAST	This sign reflects the bread being cooked on both sides.
CEREAL	This is a symbol representing CEREAL.
ORANGE+JUICE	The first part of the sign means ORANGE. When referring to the juice we add "J."
BANANA	This sign looks like peeling a banana.
MILK	This sign looks like milking a cow.
BOWL	This sign follows the shape of the BOWL.
COOK	This sign looks like cooking eggs or pancakes. You need to flip them over.
GIVE	Someone has something and gives it to another person.
TELL	This sign shows the direction of information as it is passed from one person to another.
WAITER	The first part of this compound sign means SERVE. The last part represents the PERSON who serves.
GONE	Something is no longer there.
FOOD	Well, what do you eat?
TABLE	This sign follows the physical shape of a table.
SET+TABLE	This is an action sign showing the activity of putting things on the table.
PLATE	This sign shows the shape of a plate.
GLASS	This sign shows the shape of a glass.
FORK	This sign shows the shape and use of a fork.
KNIFE	Knives are sharp. Thus, the sign KNIFE.
SPOON	This sign shows how you use a spoon.
NAPKIN	Well, how does one use a napkin?

2–11

WORK	This sign comes from the old sign for WORK and has since evolved into the present sign.
DO-WHAT	This sign started out as a fingerspelled word D-O and has evolved into a sign.
WASH	You have a plate, you take a cloth, and you scrub.
WHO	This is the symbol for the concept WHO.
HELP	Long ago this sign looked like helping someone up by the arm. It now uses a smaller movement.
MY-TURN	This sign means you are finished, now, it's my turn.
YOUR-TURN	This sign means I'm finished, now you do it.
YESTERDAY	This sign means one day in the past.
ZOOM	This shows how things become smaller as they go into the distance.

2.18 Video Learning Experience

LESSON TWO

Practice Session: Sentences

Viewing Goal: To improve your comprehension skills by watching sentences presented in ASL.

Viewing Instructions: Watch the signed sentences for comprehension. Remember to watch the face of each signer to see the facial/body expressions and the non-manual grammatical markers as well as the signs.

It is recommended that you copy each signed sentence when it is repeated.

In the space below, record any questions or notes you have regarding the sentences.

_____

_____

_____

_____

_____

_____

_____

_____

_____

2.19 Experiential Activity

What's the Sentence About?

Activity Goal: To improve your comprehension skills using sentences presented in ASL.

Activity Instructions: You will see five signed sentences. Each sentence will be signed twice. Determine what each sentence is about, and circle the correct answer below:

1. A. Asking who wants milk
   B. Asking who wants to cook
   C. Asking who wants a banana

2. A. Cooking
   B. Washing the plate
   C. Washing the glass

3. A. A food the signer loves
   B. A person the signer loves
   C. A person who loves the signer

4. A. There is no time left
   B. There are no spoons left
   C. There is no food left

5. A. Looking for food
   B. Looking for a napkin
   C. Looking for a spoon

It's Just A Drill!

2.20 Experiential Activity

Activity Goal: To improve your expressive skills by doing practice drills.

Activity Instructions: Find a partner and practice the following drills together. Remember to include non-manual question markers to show questions.

EGG, $\overline{\text{WANT}}^{\text{q}}$

FOOD,

BANANA,

MILK,

PLATE, $\overline{\text{WHO WASH}}^{\text{wh-q}}$

FORK,

SPOON,

BOWL,

GLASS,

TOAST,   GIVE-ME

NAPKIN,

KNIFE,

FOOD,

ORANGE+JUICE,   GONE

NAPKIN,

TOAST,

BOWL,

WASH PLATE,   YOUR-TURN

SET+TABLE,

HELP BABY,

WORK,

2.21 Video Learning Experience

Practice Session: Story

Viewing Goal: To improve your comprehension skills by watching a story presented in ASL.

Viewing Instructions: Watch the signed story for comprehension. In the space below, write a summary to help you remember the story.

_____

_____

_____

_____

_____

_____

_____

_____

_____

_____

2.22 Comprehension Quiz

What Did You Understand?

Quiz Goal: To see how much of the signed story you understood.

Quiz Instructions: Read and answer each question below.

1. The family in the story consisted of...
   A. A mom, dad and a son
   B. A mom and a daughter
   C. A dad, son and a daughter
   D. A mom, dad, son, and a daughter

2. _____ family member(s) were Deaf.
   A. One
   B. Two
   C. Three
   D. Five

3. The family had a _____ for a pet.
   A. Spider
   B. Cow
   C. Dog
   D. Chicken

4. In the story, who cooked breakfast?
   A. Dad
   B. Mom
   C. Anna
   D. Mom and Anna

5. Why didn't Anna eat?
   A. She doesn't like Dad's cooking.
   B. The dog had taken a bite out of her food.
   C. She wasn't hungry yet.
   D. She was late for school.

6. What did Anna do with her breakfast food?

   _____

7. Later on, what happened to Anna at school?

   _____

2.23 Homework Assignment

Did You Hear The One About Breakfast?

Homework Goal: To help you improve your ASL expressive skills.

Homework Instructions: Create a story about your family having breakfast. The story must include at least eight of the ASL vocabulary introduced in this lesson. Also use at least three adjectives or signs modified in ways demonstrated in the *Grammatical Notes* section.

2.24 Post-test Introduction

What Do You Know Now?

Post-test Goal: To assess your mastery of the lesson objectives.

Post-test Introduction: This test has three sections:

Section One: The Comprehension section tests your ability to understand ASL.

Section Two: The Culture and Grammar section tests your knowledge of the material presented in the *Cultural* and *Grammatical Notes*.

Section Three: The Expressive portion tests your ability to use ASL.

Simply follow the instructions for each section.

Good Luck!

LESSON TWO

Lesson 3
WHERE'S THE TV REMOTE?

3.2 Homework Review

Did You Hear the One About Breakfast?

Activity Goal: To show what you did for homework.

Activity Instructions: Find a partner and take turns signing the story you were assigned in Lesson Two.

Remember to include at least eight of the ASL vocabulary introduced in Lesson Two and at least three adjectives or sign modifications.

When your partner is signing, pay close attention and practice your ASL comprehension skills! Use ASL to ask questions about your partner's story.

3.3 Pretest

What Do You Know?

Pretest Goal: To see how much you already know about what will be taught in this lesson.

Pretest Instructions: Read each question and circle the best answers.

1. How do Deaf people gain access to telecommunication? (Circle all that apply.)
   A. Captions on the television
   B. Flashing lights
   C. Technology such as; internet, email and video communication, etc.
   D. Video relay Service (VRS)

---

2. If there is a hearing person living in the home;
   A. Visual modifications are not necessary
   B. The hearing person can answer the phone and door
   C. The hearing person can tell the others what is happening
   D. The home needs to be totally accessible to everyone equally

3. A relay service can help a hearing person who does not know sign language or have the technology needed to call a Deaf person.
   A. True
   B. False

4. In ASL, a simple side-to-side headshake can turn a positive statement into a negative.
   A. True
   B. False

5. In ASL, negation is always indicated at the beginning of the sentence for clarity.
   A. True
   B. False

3.4 Lesson Objectives

Planning for Success

Goal: To see what you will learn by the end of this lesson.

Instructions: Read the objectives below.

Upon completing this VideoCourse lesson, you will be able to...

1. Recognize and accurately produce the ASL vocabulary introduced in this and all previous lessons.

2. Name and describe several ways in which Deaf people make the sounds in their homes visible to gain more access and independence.

3. Describe how Deaf people can access the telephone.

4. Recognize how negation is demonstrated in ASL.

5. Recognize the "use of space" features of ASL addressed in this lesson.

3.5 Lesson Focus

Which Way Did it Go?

Activity Goal: To practice giving directions without using your voice.

Activity Instructions: One student will be the "seeker" and leave the room while an item is hidden somewhere in the classroom. Your job is to give the seeker clues - using mime and gestures - to help the seeker find the item.

To add to the fun, do not use your voice, point, or look in the direction of the object. Once the object is found, a new seeker will be selected. Good luck!

Thought/Discussion Questions

1. What are some signs related to giving directions that would have been useful to know during this activity?

_____

_____

_____

_____

2. How did it feel to be limited in your ability to communicate?

_____

_____

_____

_____

3. What are some techniques that Deaf people could use in giving directions to people who do not sign?

_____

_____

_____

_____

3.6 Language Learning Instruction

Learning New Signs

Goal: To help you learn new ASL vocabulary.

Instructions: Your instructor will teach you new signs! Watch closely to learn what these signs mean and how they are produced.

In the space below, record any notes to help you remember the signs.

_____

_____

_____

_____

_____

_____

_____

_____

_____

_____

3.7 Video Learning Experience

LESSON THREE

Introduction to New Vocabulary

Viewing Goal: To help you learn the new ASL vocabulary.

Viewing Instructions: Watch how Billy produces each sign. Be sure to notice the facial/body expressions. Copy the signs as Billy repeats each one.

Signs representing the following concepts are introduced in this video segment:

1. REMOTE-CONTROL
2. CHAIR
3. COUCH
4. LIVING+ROOM
5. T-V
6. ON
7. UNDER
8. BEHIND
9. IN
10. BED+ROOM
11. BED
12. DRESSER
13. UPSTAIRS

3.8
Experiential
Activity

Matchmaker

Activity Goal: To help you recognize the new ASL vocabulary.

Activity Instructions: Look at the illustrations of your new ASL vocabulary below. Draw a line from the illustration of the sign to the picture that best matches its meaning.

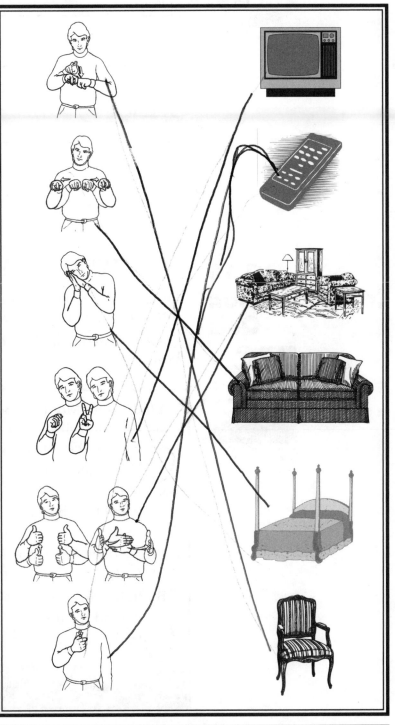

3.9 Video Learning Experience

Bravo Family Visit

Viewing Goal: To improve your ASL comprehension by watching a Bravo family interaction.

Viewing Instructions: Watch the signed interaction and write a summary of the main points.

_____

_____

_____

_____

_____

_____

_____

_____

_____

3.10 Comprehension Quiz

What Did You Understand?

Quiz Goal: To see how much of the Bravo family interaction you understood.

Quiz Instructions: Read each question and circle the best answer.

1. Where does Mom ask Scott to look for the TV remote control?

   A. Next to the couch.

   B. Under the couch.

   C. In the bed.

   D. All of the above.

2. Where does Anna look for the remote control?

   A. In the closet.

   B. In the dresser.

   C. Behind the door.

   D. In the bed.

---

3. Where does Anna find the remote control?
   A. Under the bed.
   B. Inside the bed.
   C. On the dresser.
   D. She doesn't find it.
4. Where does Scott find the remote?
   A. Under the couch.
   B. Behind the chair.
   C. In the kitchen.
   D. He doesn't find it.

3.11 Language Learning Instruction

Learning New Signs

Goal: To help you learn new ASL vocabulary.

Instructions: Your instructor will teach you new signs! Watch closely to learn what these signs mean and how they are produced.

In the space below, record any notes to help you remember the signs.

_____
_____
_____
_____
_____
_____
_____
_____
_____
_____

3.12 Video Learning Experience

Introduction to New Vocabulary

Viewing Goal: To help you learn new ASL vocabulary.

Viewing Instructions: Watch how Billy produces each sign. Be sure to notice the facial/body expressions. Copy the signs as Billy repeats each one.

Signs representing the following concepts are introduced in this video segment:

1. OVEN
2. REFRIGERATOR
3. SINK
4. TTY/TDD

5. TELEPHONE
6. LIGHT
7. FLASHING-LIGHT
8. BATH

3.13 Experiential Activity

Put it There, Pal!

Activity Goal: To help you recognize the new ASL vocabulary and the spatial features of ASL.

Activity Instructions: Watch the video and put an "X" where the signer tells you to on each of the pictures below.

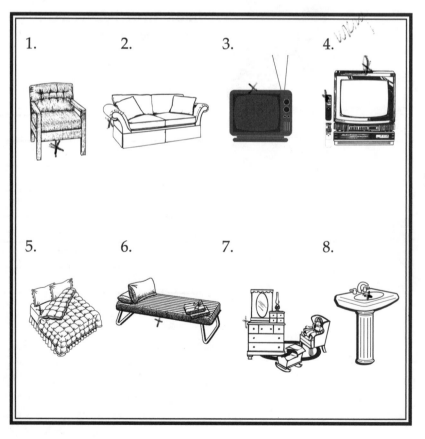

3.14 Video Learning Experience

LESSON THREE

Bravo Family Visit

Viewing Goal: To improve your ASL comprehension skills by watching a Bravo family interaction.

Viewing Instructions: Watch the signed interaction and write a summary of the main points.

_____

_____

_____

_____

_____

_____

_____

3.15 Comprehension Quiz

Ringing haven't not all my fault

What Did You Understand?

Quiz Goal: To see how much of the Bravo family interaction you understood.

Quiz Instructions: Read and answer each question below.

1. Why did Mom think the TV remote control might be in the bathroom?
   Children

2. What did it mean when the light flashed?
   phone ring

3. When Anna came into the room after the light flashed, what did she ask Mom?
   phone 4 me

4. When Mom found Dad in the bathroom, what was he doing?
   looking in shower

5. Anna is still on the phone when Mom passes her. What does Mom tell her?

   A. "Say hello to your friend for me."

   B. "Let me talk to your friend's mother."

   C. "Time to take the dog for a walk."

   D. "Time to end your phone conversation."

6. Where did the Bravo family find the remote control?

   cushins

7. What did Scott say when the family looked at him accusingly?

   A. "It's not my fault, you didn't tell me to look there!"

   B. "I fooled you! I hid it there!"

   C. "I didn't want to watch TV anyway!"

   D. "Anna told me to put it there!"

3.16 Video Learning Experience

LESSON THREE

Cultural Notes

Viewing Goal: To learn about the cultural aspects of ASL.

Viewing Instructions: View the *Cultural Notes* segment carefully for the following:

The sounds in Deaf people's homes are made accessible with:

   A. Flashing lights that identify audible signals such as:

     1. Doorbell

     2. Fire alarm

     3. Baby crying

     4. Alarm clock

     5. Telephone ringing

   B. Hearing dogs that are specially trained to alert Deaf people to environmental sounds.

   C. Captions that make the audio from the TV accessible.

LESSON
THREE

3.17
Experiential
Activity

Home Improvement

Activity Goal: To apply the cultural information you have learned about accessibility for Deaf people.

Activity Instructions: Read each situation below and consider what steps could be taken to ensure accessibility within each. For each situation, decide what visual modifications could be applied. Write your ideas and suggestions below.

Situation 1: A Deaf woman wants to start a business taking care of infants/children in her home.

_____

_____

Situation 2: A Deaf man needs to make a telephone call to his Deaf friend.

_____

_____

Situation 3: Your Deaf sister isn't waking up in time for school.

_____

_____

Situation 4: A Deaf girl needs to make a telephone call to her hearing friend.

_____

_____

Situation 5: A Deaf person is expecting a visit from a friend.

_____

_____

Situation 6: A Deaf college student needs to remain up-to-date with current world events.

_____

_____

TDD   GA Go ahead
to
SK   stop Key

sign off SKSK

LESSON THREE

Thought/Discussion Questions

1. What would be the cost of some of your recommendations for access?
   _____
   _____

2. Who should pay these costs?
   _____
   _____

3. Think about how it would be if you were Deaf... how would you gain access to educational opportunities, emergency medical care, movies and theater, social events, etc.?
   _____
   _____

4. If you were Deaf, what adjustments would you make in your own home?
   _____
   _____

3.18 Video Learning Experience

LESSON THREE

Negation

Negative @ end of sentence w/ head shake.

*no
can't
won't
don't*

Grammatical Notes

Viewing Goal: To learn about the grammatical aspects of ASL.

Viewing Instructions: View the *Grammatical Notes* segment carefully for the following:

How negation is demonstrated in ASL:

A. ASL tends to place the sign indicating a negative at the end of the signed sentence.

B. A negative headshake accompanies the sign indicating negation.

3.19 Experiential Activity

To Be, or NOT To Be

Activity Goal: To practice identifying whether an ASL sentence is affirmative (positive) or negative.

Activity Instructions: You will see ten sentences signed in ASL. The sentences are either affirmative or negative. After viewing each sentence, circle the appropriate response below.

1. AFFIRMATIVE | NEGATIVE
2. AFFIRMATIVE | NEGATIVE
3. AFFIRMATIVE | NEGATIVE
4. AFFIRMATIVE | NEGATIVE
5. AFFIRMATIVE | NEGATIVE
6. AFFIRMATIVE | NEGATIVE
7. AFFIRMATIVE | NEGATIVE
8. AFFIRMATIVE | NEGATIVE
9. AFFIRMATIVE | NEGATIVE
10. AFFIRMATIVE | NEGATIVE

3.20 Video Learning Experience

LESSON THREE

Review Session

Viewing Goal: To help you remember how to produce the signs introduced in this lesson.

Viewing Instructions: Watch this video segment carefully to see how each sign is made, and take note of any hints given to help you remember. You may want to copy the signs as you watch Billy.

The following are the vocabulary and explanations offered in this video segment:

CHAIR	This sign shows that a chair is something you sit on.
COUCH	This looks like several chairs next to each other... showing that several people can sit on it at the same time.
TV	This is fingerspelled T-V.
REMOTE-CONTROL	This sign shows both the shape and function of a remote control.
ON	The left hand becomes the surface of a thing. The right hand shows that something is ON it.
UNDER	The left hand is an object, the right hand shows the location of another thing UNDER it.
BEHIND	One thing is located BEHIND another.
IN	This sign shows the location of IN/INSIDE.
OVEN	This sign reflects the activity of putting something in an oven.
REFRIGERATOR	This compound sign shows how you OPEN it and indicates that it is COLD.
SINK	This sign indicates the basic shape and how you use a sink.
BED+ROOM	This is a compound sign using the signs BED and ROOM.
TOILET/BATHROOM	This is a symbol for BATHROOM. The "T" represents the letter in the word TOILET.
BED	This sign represents someone's head on the pillow.
DRESSER	This sign is based on the shape and function of a dresser.
BATH	You take a washcloth and soap and you scrub away.
PHONE	This is a sign indicating a phone's shape and use.

TTY — This is a device the phone is placed on. One types the conversation so it becomes visible.

LIGHT — The hand becomes the light bulb and the fingers represent the LIGHT.

FLASHING-LIGHT — The hand is the bulb, and the fingers show the light going on and off.

3.21 Video Learning Experience

LESSON THREE

Practice Session: Sentences

Viewing Goal: To improve your ASL comprehension skills by watching signed sentences.

Viewing Instructions: Watch the signed sentences for comprehension. Remember to watch the face of each signer to see the facial/body expressions and the non-manual grammatical markers as well as the signs. It is recommended that you copy each signed sentence when it is repeated.

In the space below, record any questions or notes you have regarding the sentences.

_____

_____

_____

_____

_____

3.22 Experiential Activity

Now, Where Did I Put That...?

Activity Goal: To improve your comprehension skills with the spatial features of ASL.

Activity Instructions: You will see signed directions that tell you where in the house (see picture below) the ten items belong. Place the number corresponding to the item in the correct location in the house. If, for example, in item #1 the signer informs you, "the glass is on the table," you would write "1" on the table in the picture.

1. GLASS	6. DOG
2. REMOTE-CONTROL	7. SPIDER
3. COFFEE	8. TELEPHONE
4. BANANA	9. TTY
5. EGG	10. MILK

LESSON
THREE

3.23 Experiential Activity

You Want Me to Do What?

Activity Goal: To improve your comprehension and your ability to recognize the spatial features of ASL.

Activity Instructions: Pay close attention as your instructor signs commands for the students to follow. When you are selected, complete the task signed to you in ASL.

Practice giving and receiving commands with a classmate.

3.24 Video Learning Experience

Practice Session: Story

Viewing Goal: To improve your ASL comprehension by watching a story presented in ASL.

Viewing Instructions: Watch the signed story for comprehension. In the space below, write a summary of the main points from the story.

_____

_____

_____

_____

_____

_____

_____

_____

_____

_____

3.25 Comprehension Quiz

What Did You Understand?

Quiz Goal: To see how much of the signed story you understood.

Quiz Instructions: Read each question below and choose the best answer.

1. How many bedrooms does the house in the story have?
   A. One
   B. Two
   C. Three
   D. Four

2. The house in the story was unusual because it did not have a kitchen.
   A. True
   B. False

3. According to the story, where should you go if you are hungry?
   A. Since there is no kitchen, to a restaurant
   B. To a neighbor's house
   C. To the kitchen
   D. To a friend's house

4 According to this story, if a light is flashing, where should you go?
   A. To the bathroom
   B. To the bedroom
   C. To the front door
   D. To the phone

5. In this story, if you want to watch TV, where should you go?
   A. The bedroom
   B. The TV room
   C. The living room
   D. A hardware store to buy a new remote control

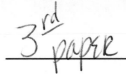

3.26 Homework Assignment

(handwritten notes in left margin:)

1. TV

2. Get closed captions 2work

3. Program
   DeafClub
   culture 50-50 ticket
   go to have to go 2 meeting

Read Any Good TV Lately?

Homework Goal: To give you an opportunity to experience access to television through captions.

Homework Instructions: Find a television that has a built-in caption decoder or visit a friend who has one. Watch your favorite television program or movie *without the sound* by reading the captions.

Write a one- to three-page paper describing your experience including:

A. Was it easy to access closed captions?

B. Was the program you wanted to watch accessible with captions or English subtitles?

C. What was it like to view the program with captions instead of sound?

D. Were you able to read the captions and view all the action?

(handwritten:) 5th point

3.27 Post-test Introduction

What Do You Know Now?

Post-test Goal: To assess your mastery of the lesson objectives.

Post-test Introduction: This test has three sections:

Section One: The Comprehension section tests your ability to understand ASL.

Section Two: The Culture and Grammar section tests your knowledge of the material presented in the *Cultural* and *Grammatical Notes.*

Section Three: The Expressive portion tests your ability to use ASL.

Simply follow the instructions for each section.

Good luck!

Lesson 4
LET'S GO FOOD SHOPPING

4.2 Homework Review

Read Any Good TV Lately?

Activity Goal: To share the results of your homework assignment.

Activity Instructions: Be prepared to share the main points from your paper regarding watching television with captions including:

A. Was it easy to access closed captions?

B. Was the program you wanted to watch accessible with captions?

C. What was it like to view the program with captions instead of sound?

D. Were you able to read the captions and view all the action?

4.3 Pretest

What Do You Know?

Pretest Goal: To see how much you already know about what will be taught in this lesson.

Pretest Instructions: Read each question and circle the best answer.

---

1. ASL is often creative and imaginative.

   A. True
   B. False

2. ASL can make a "play on signs" like English can make a "play on words."

   A. True
   B. False

---

3. ASL and English have the same word order.

    A. True
    B. False

4. In ASL, the topic of a sentence is often signed first

    A. True
    B. False

5. ASL has rules of grammar just like spoken languages

    A. True
    B. False

6. A Number Story is always limited to two minutes.

    A. True
    B. False

4.4 Lesson Objectives

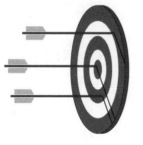

Planning For Success

Goal: To see what you will learn by the end of this lesson.

Instructions: Read the objectives below.

Upon completing this VideoCourse lesson, you will be able to...

1. Recognize and accurately produce the ASL vocabulary introduced in this and all previous lessons.

2. Describe a Number Story as a form of Deaf folklore and contribute to the creation of an original Number Story.

3. Name and describe several ways in which Deaf people share the folklore of Deaf culture.

4. Recognize and apply topic/comment grammatical structure.

4.5 Lesson Focus

Where's The Beef?

Activity Goal: To experience a situational role-play related to food shopping.

Activity Instructions: Imagine that you are in a grocery store. The store is owned by a Deaf family and the language used in the store is ASL. You need help to find certain items.

Role-play this situation in your group and think of how you might request the location of the following twelve items using gestures and mime.

Use the space provided below to list your ideas. Be creative! Although you may not know the signs for the items, try to overcome the communication barrier by using natural gestures/body movements to "act out" each item.

You need the following food items:

1. Soda	4. Popcorn	7. Chicken	10. Eggs
2. Milk	5. Lobster	8. Dog food	11. Eggplant
3. Soup	6. Bananas	9. Fish	12. Hamburger

Communication ideas:

1. _____   7._____

2. _____   8._____

3. _____   9._____

4. _____ 10._____

5. _____ 11._____

6. _____ 12._____

In this lesson, you will learn the signs for the above food items and more. Next time you need something from this grocery store, you will be ready!

LESSON FOUR

Thought/Discussion Questions

1. What are some signs related to food that would have been useful to know during this activity?

_____

_____

_____

_____

2. How did it feel to be limited in your ability to communicate?

_____

_____

_____

_____

3. What are some ways that Deaf people could ask for the location of items in a food store?

_____

_____

_____

_____

4.6 Language Learning Instruction

Learning New Signs

Goal: To help you learn new ASL vocabulary.

Instructions: Your instructor will teach you new signs! Watch closely to learn what these signs mean and how they are produced.

In the space below, record any notes to help you remember the signs.

_____

_____

_____

_____

_____

_____

_____

_____

_____

4.7 Video Learning Experience

Introduction to New Vocabulary

Viewing Goal: To help you learn the new ASL vocabulary.

Viewing Instructions: As the family shops, they will show you new signs. Watch how each sign is produced. Be sure to notice the facial/body expressions.

During the food shopping trip, signs representing the following concepts are introduced:

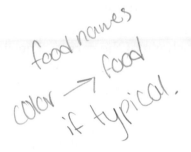

food names
color → food
if typical.

1. SODA/POP	14. CHEESE	27. CANDY
2. ALL-GONE	15. HOT-DOG	28. COOKIES
3. FOOD	16. HAMBURGER	29. ICE-CREAM
4. SHOPPING	17. TURKEY	30. # 1
5. BANANA	18. FISH	31. # 2
6. MELON	19. CHICKEN	32. # 3
7. PLANT	20. BREAD	33. # 4
8. EGG+PLANT	21. POPCORN	34. # 5
9. LETTUCE	22. KETCHUP	35. # 6
10. ONION	23. SOUP	36. # 7
11. CARROT	24. TOMATO	37. # 8
12. COW	25. DOG+FOOD	38. # 9
13. MILK	26. LOBSTER	39. # 10

4.8 Video Learning Experience

Review Session

Viewing Goal: To help you remember how to produce the signs introduced in this lesson.

Viewing Instructions: Watch this video segment carefully to see how each sign is made, and take note of any hints given to help you remember. You may want to copy the signs as you watch Billy.

The following are the vocabulary and explanations offered in this video segment:

SODA/POP — This sign looks like opening a soda can.

ALL-GONE — The left hand represents a pile of things. The right hand shows the depletion of those things.

FOOD — Where does the food go? In the mouth.

SHOPPING	The sign BUY is like taking money out of your hand and giving it to someone. When you repeat the sign several times (to buy many things), you are... SHOPPING.
BANANA	This sign looks like peeling a banana.
MELON	How do you test a melon to see if it's good? You thump it.
PLANT	This sign looks like something growing up out of the ground.
EGG+PLANT	This is a compound sign using EGG and PLANT. This vegetable is shaped similar to an egg.
LETTUCE	The head becomes the plant itself and the right hand represents a leaf.
ONION	When you're eating or chopping an onion, your eyes water.
CARROT	The index finger shows the shape of the carrot. The right hand represents the action of peeling the carrot.
COW	This clearly represents an animal with horns.
MILK	This sign looks like milking a cow.
CHEESE	To make cheese, milk is processed and becomes solid. This sign represents the compressed liquid becoming CHEESE.
HOT-DOG	This sign represents how the hot dogs are made.
HAMBURGER	This shows how a person makes a hamburger patty.
TURKEY:	This describes what a turkey looks like, specifically its wattle.
FISH	The hand becomes a fish swimming.
CHICKEN	This sign looks like a chicken's beak.
BREAD	You have a loaf of bread, and you slice it.
POPCORN	When cooked, popcorn kernels explode and pop up.
KETCHUP	Most people hit the bottle to get the ketchup out.
SOUP	The left hand represents the bowl. The right hand represents the spoon.
TOMATO	The first part of the sign means RED. The left hand becomes the tomato, while the right hand slices it.
DOG+FOOD	This is a compound sign using the signs for DOG and FOOD.
LOBSTER	This sign clearly depicts a lobster's claws.
CANDY	This sign shows the candy in the mouth.
COOKIES	This looks like a cookie cutter when making cookies.
ICE-CREAM	This sign shows the way a person licks an ice cream cone.

4.9 Experiential Activity

Con-SIGN-tration

Activity Goal: To help you recognize and produce the new ASL vocabulary.

Activity Instructions: Your class will be divided into two teams and will play a game called "Con-SIGN-tration."

One person will go to the board and select a Con-SIGN-tration card. This student must sign the vocabulary item that best represents the picture to the class. If the sign is correct and produced accurately, s/he selects a second card. If the pictures match, his/her team gets a point and another student from the same team gets a turn.

If there is no match, or the signs are not produced correctly, the other team gets a turn.

Have fun and remember to con-SIGN-trate!

4.10 Experiential Activity

Don't Forget to Buy the...!

Activity Goal: To help you recognize the new ASL vocabulary.

Activity Instructions: You are going food shopping for three of your friends. Watch the video carefully as each one tells you what s/he wants you to buy at the grocery store. Circle the pictures of each of the items they sign so you don't forget!

Friend #1 wants you to buy...

Friend #2 wants you to buy...

Friend #3 wants you to buy...

4.11 Video Learning Experience

LESSON FOUR

Practice Session: Sentences

Viewing Goal: To improve your comprehension skills by watching sentences presented in ASL.

Viewing Instructions: Watch the signed sentences for comprehension. Remember to watch the face of each signer to see the facial/body expressions and the non-manual grammatical signals as well as the signs.

It is recommended that you copy each signed sentence when it is repeated.

In the space below, record any questions or notes you have regarding the sentences.

_____

_____

_____

_____

4.12 Experiential Activity

What's the Sentence About?

Activity Goal: To improve your comprehension skills using sentences presented in ASL.

Activity Instructions: You will see five signed sentences. Each sentence will be signed twice. Determine what each sentence is about, and circle the correct answer below:

1. A. Watching fireworks
   B. Wanting lobster
   C. Wanting popcorn

2. A. Buying carrots
   B. Buying onions
   C. Eating cheese

3. A. Making soup
   B. Cooking onions
   C. Eating onions

4. A. Watching TV
   B. Watching me
   C. Eating TV dinners

5. A. Being good
   B. Being tired
   C. Being hungry

4.13 Video Learning Experience

LESSON FOUR

Cultural Notes

Viewing Goal: To learn about the cultural aspects of ASL.

Viewing Instructions: View the *Cultural Notes* segment carefully for the following:

ASL storytelling is often creative and imaginative.

1. One example of this is the creation of Number Stories that use only the handshapes of numbers to tell the story.

2. Billy demonstrates a story using only the handshapes for numbers 1-10. The story is entitled "The Grocery Store Cashier." Billy explains the components of the story as:

Handshape:	What each handshape means:
1	A person working (a grocery store cashier)
2	The green bow tie worn by the cashier
3	The items being purchased
4	The clerk ringing up the prices on the register
5	A physical characteristic of the cashier (her hair)
6	The big bow in her hair
7	The cashier broke a fingernail
8	The cashier using a nail file
9	Her eyes turning to notice something
10	Many people waiting in line

Note: Following the explanation, Billy performs the whole story (see activity 4.14).

4.14 Video Learning Experience

LESSON FOUR

The Food Store Cashier

Viewing Goal: To see an example of a Number Story performed.

Viewing Instructions: Watch Billy perform the Number Story. Notice the handshapes he uses in the story.

In the space below, record any questions or notes regarding the performance.

_____

_____

_____

_____

_____

_____

_____

_____

4.15 Experiential Activity

Simple as One, Two, Three!

Activity Goal: To create a Number Story.

Activity Instructions: You and your classmates will create a Number Story similar to the one demonstrated by Billy. Be creative, but remember to only use the handshapes of the numbers 1-10!

Don't worry; if you get stuck, your teacher will help you! When the story is complete, you will be given a chance to practice signing the story.

Use the lines below to record notes about what each number represents to help you remember the story.

Handshape:	What each handshape means:
1	_____
2	_____
3	_____
4	_____
5	_____
6	_____
7	_____
8	_____
9	_____
10	_____

4.16 Video Learning Experience

Grammatical Notes

Viewing Goal: To learn about the grammatical aspects of ASL.

Viewing Instructions: View the *Grammatical Notes* segment carefully for the following:

I. ASL Grammatical Structure:

    A. ASL sentence structure is different from English.

    B. ASL has many grammatical rules.

    C. A commonly used structure is that of "topic/comment" structure.

II. Topic/Comment Structure:

A. In ASL, the topic of the sentence (what the sentence is about) is signed first.

B. The comment (what you want to say about the topic) is signed after the topic. Here are some examples:

1. In English, we say "three carrots." In ASL, first the topic is established, CARROT, then the comment follows, THREE.

2. ONION, (the topic) FOUR (the comment) is demonstrated by Anna at the food store.

C. Some of the ways the topic of a sentence is identified:

1. Eyebrows raised

2. The last sign of the topic is held longer

3. There is a slight head-tilt

Note: Watch for these topic markers to help you recognize the topics of sentences structured this way.

Topic Search

4.17 Experiential Activity

Activity Goal: To identify the topic within sentences presented in ASL.

Activity Instructions: You will see five sentences signed in ASL. For each sentence, circle the topic.

1. I love mother.

2. There are four hotdogs.

3. I love popcorn.

4. I want some milk.

5. The children are hungry.

4.18 Video Learning Experience

LESSON FOUR

Practice Session: Story

Viewing Goal: To improve your comprehension skills by watching a story presented in ASL.

Viewing Instructions: Watch the signed story for comprehension. In the space below, write a summary to help you remember the story.

_____

_____

_____

_____

_____

_____

_____

_____

_____

_____

_____

_____

4.19
Comprehension
Quiz

What Did You Understand?

Quiz Goal: To see how much of the signed story you understood.

Quiz Instructions: Read and answer each question below.

1. What did the family in the story do?
   - A. Go grocery shopping
   - B. Go to the movies
   - C. Cook breakfast
   - D. Clean the house

2. _____ wanted to go alone, but everyone wanted to help.
   - A. Scott
   - B. Mom
   - C. Dad
   - D. Anna

3. Scott likes to go food shopping.
   - A. True
   - B. False

4. Name at least three things the family bought.
   onions , carrots , milk

5. What did Scott buy?
   Candy, Ice cream, cookies

4.20 Homework Assignment

A Food Shopping Adventure

Homework Goal: To improve your ASL expressive skills.

Homework Instructions: Create a signed story about your family going food shopping. Use at least ten of the vocabulary items introduced in this lesson. Be sure to also include at least two sentences using topic/comment structure as taught in the *Grammatical Notes*.

Be prepared to sign your story to the class.

4.21 Post-test Introduction

What Do You Know Now?

Post-test Goal: To assess your mastery of the lesson objectives.

Post-test Introduction: This test has three sections.

Section One: The Comprehension section tests your ability to understand ASL.

Section Two: The Culture and Grammar section tests your knowledge of the material presented in the *Cultural* and *Grammatical Notes*.

Section Three: The Expressive portion tests your ability to use ASL.

Simply follow the instructions for each section.

Good luck!

4–15

Lesson 5
REVIEW & PRACTICE SESSION

5.2 Homework Review

A Food Shopping Adventure

Activity Goal: To show the results of your homework assignment.

Activity Instructions: Find a partner and take turns signing the story, *A Food Shopping Adventure*, that was assigned in Lesson Four. Remember to use at least ten of the ASL vocabulary items introduced in Lesson Four and at least two sentences using topic/comment structure.

When your partner is signing, pay close attention and practice your ASL comprehension skills! Use ASL to ask questions about your partner's story.

Be prepared to sign your story to the class.

5.3 Lesson Objectives

Planning for Success

Goal: To see what you will learn by the end of this lesson.

Instructions: Read the objectives below.

Upon completing this VideoCourse lesson, you will be able to...

1. Recognize and accurately produce the ASL vocabulary introduced in Lessons One, Two, Three, and Four.

2. Demonstrate knowledge of the cultural information presented in Lessons One, Two, Three, and Four.

3. Recognize and apply the grammatical features presented in Lessons One, Two, Three, and Four.

4. Accurately use the ASL vocabulary and grammatical features presented in Lessons One, Two, Three, and Four in sentences, dialogues, and stories.

5.4 Video Learning Experience

LESSON FIVE

Lesson Introduction

Viewing Goal: To help you prepare for this review session.

Viewing Instructions: Watch carefully as Billy explains what you can expect from this *Review & Practice Session.*

Pay attention to what he is signing, but also notice *how* he expresses these ideas. Perhaps you will learn a few more signs! Watch how Billy uses facial/body expression, non-manual grammatical markers, and use of space.

In the space below, write any notes or questions you may have.

_____

_____

_____

_____

_____

_____

_____

_____

5.5 Experiential Activity

Crossword Puzzle

Activity Goal: To help you remember the ASL vocabulary learned in Lesson One.

Activity Instructions: You will see several ASL vocabulary items from Lesson One signed on the video, as well as each answer's location on the puzzle, for example: 1 Across - MOTHER.

Decide what English word describes what is being signed and fits in the puzzle. Write it in the correct boxes. Each sign will be presented twice.

5.6 Video Learning Experience

LESSON FIVE

Lesson One Review: Vocabulary

Viewing Goal: To help you review the ASL vocabulary from Lesson One.

Viewing Instructions: Watch the Lesson One vocabulary review while you copy the signs. Raise your hand if there is a sign you do not remember, and your instructor will help you.

Signs representing the following concepts are reviewed in this video segment:

1. MOM/MOTHER	13. DEAF	25. DOG
2. CHILDREN	14. HEARING	26. FOOL-YOU
3. BABY	15. WHICH	27. SHOWER
4. GOOD	16. WANT	28. KITCHEN
5. MORNING	17. TOILET/BATHROOM	29. SON
6. COFFEE	18. BRUSH-TEETH	30. DAUGHTER
7. HUNGRY	19. TIME	31. SCARED/AFRAID
8. YES	20. WAKE-UP	32. BED
9. NO	21. SCHOOL	33. SPIDER
10. THANK-YOU	22. BREAKFAST	34. ALMOST
11. WHERE	23. PAST/BEFORE	35. GET-DRESSED
12. LOVE	24. GO	

5.7 Video Learning Experience

LESSON FIVE

Lesson One Review: Sentences

Viewing Goal: To improve your comprehension skills by watching sentences presented in ASL.

Viewing Instructions: Watch the signed sentences for comprehension. Remember to watch the face of each signer to see the facial/body expressions, non-manual grammatical markers, and the signs.

It is recommended that you copy each signed sentence when it is repeated.

_____

_____

_____

_____

_____

_____

_____

_____

_____

_____

5.8 Video Learning Experience

LESSON FIVE

Lesson One Review: Practice Dialogue

Viewing Goal: To improve your comprehension skills by watching a dialogue presented in ASL.

Viewing Instructions: Watch the signed dialogue for comprehension and take notes or write a summary in the space provided.

_____

_____

_____

_____

_____

_____

_____

_____

5.9 Experiential Activity

Dynamic-Duo Dialogue

Activity Goal: To improve your expressive and receptive ASL skills.

Activity Instructions: Work with a partner to create a dialogue using the Lesson One vocabulary (see the Sign Illustration Section for Lesson One vocabulary). Use ASL (no voices needed!) and be sure each person takes at least three turns signing.

Be prepared to share your dialogue with the class!

In the space below, record any ideas or notes you have regarding the dialogue.

_____

_____

_____

_____

_____

_____

_____

_____

5.10 Video Learning Experience

Bravo Family Revisited

Viewing Goal: To reinforce your ASL receptive and expressive skills by reviewing a Bravo family interaction from Lesson One.

Viewing Instructions: Watch the *Bravo Family Revisited* for review.

Be prepared to re-enact this scene (using ASL) with your classmates!

_____

_____

_____

_____

_____

_____

5.11 Experiential Activity

It's Your Turn to Set the Table!

Activity Goal: To help you remember the ASL vocabulary learned in Lesson Two.

Activity Instructions: With a partner, take turns using ASL to describe setting the table for breakfast. Use as many of the Lesson Two signs as possible. (See the Illustration Section for Lesson Two vocabulary.)

5.12 Video Learning Experience

Lesson Two Review: Vocabulary

Viewing Goal: To help you review the ASL vocabulary from Lesson Two.

Viewing Instructions: Watch the Lesson Two vocabulary review while you copy the signs. Raise your hand if there is a sign you do not remember, and your instructor will help you.

Signs representing the following concepts are reviewed in this video segment:

1. COOK	11. GIVE	21. NAPKIN
2. EAT	12. TELL	22. WORK
3. EGG	13. WAITER	23. DO-WHAT
4. TOAST	14. GONE	24. WASH
5. CEREAL	15. SET+TABLE	25. HELP
6. ORANGE+JUICE	16. PLATE	26. MY-TURN
7. BANANA	17. GLASS	27. YOUR-TURN
8. MILK	18. FORK	28. YESTERDAY
9. ONE	19. KNIFE	
10. TWO	20. SPOON	

5.13 Video Learning Experience

Lesson Two Review: Sentences

Viewing Goal: To improve your comprehension skills by watching sentences presented in ASL.

Viewing Instructions: Watch the signed sentences for comprehension. Remember to watch the face of each signer to see the facial/body expressions and the non-manual grammatical markers as well as the signs. It is recommended that you copy each signed sentence when it is repeated.

_____

_____

_____

5.14 Video Learning Experience

Lesson Two Review: Practice Dialogue

Viewing Goal: To improve your comprehension skills by watching a dialogue presented in ASL.

Viewing Instructions: Watch the signed dialogue for comprehension and answer the questions below.

1. Where is the spider?

_____

2. How does Scott feel about spiders?

_____

3. How does Mom feel about spiders?

_____

4. What does Scott want to do with a fork?

    A. Eat the spider.
    B. Eat breakfast.
    C. Fling the spider.
    D. Kill the spider.

5. What does Mom want to do with the glass?

    A. Drink the spider.
    B. Capture the spider.
    C. Drink water.
    D. Drink milk.

5.15 Experiential Activity

Dynamic-Duo Dialogue

Activity Goal: To improve your expressive and receptive ASL skills.

Activity Instructions: Work with a partner to create a dialogue using the Lesson Two vocabulary (see the Sign Illustration Section for Lesson Two vocabulary). Use ASL (no voices needed!) and be sure each person takes at least three turns signing. Be prepared to share your dialogue with the class!

In the space below, record any ideas or notes you have regarding the dialogue.

_____

_____

_____

_____

_____

_____

_____

_____

5.16 Video Learning Experience

Bravo Family Revisited

Viewing Goal: To reinforce your ASL receptive and expressive skills by reviewing a Bravo family interaction from Lesson Two.

Viewing Instructions: Watch the *Bravo Family Revisited* for review. Be prepared to re-enact this scene (using ASL) with your classmates!

_____

_____

_____

_____

_____

_____

_____

_____

5.17
Experiential
Activity

Matchmaker

Activity Goal: To help you remember some of the ASL vocabulary learned in Lesson Three.

Activity Instructions: Look at the illustrations of the Lesson Three vocabulary below. Draw a line from the illustration of the sign to the picture that best matches its meaning.

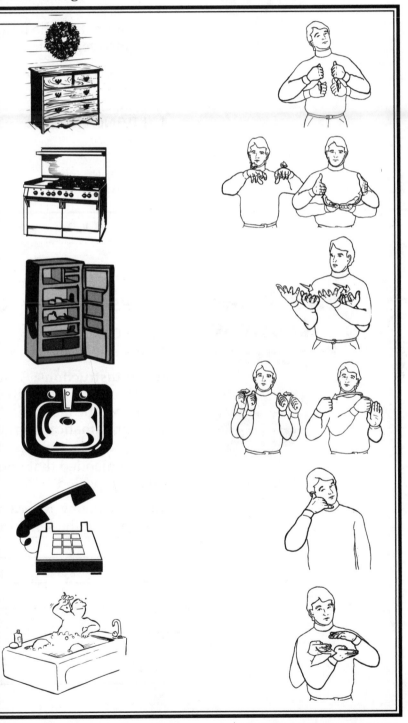

5.18 Video Learning Experience

Lesson Three Review: Vocabulary

Viewing Goal: To help you review the ASL vocabulary from Lesson Three.

Viewing Instructions: Watch the Lesson Three vocabulary review while you copy the signs. Raise your hand if there is a sign you do not remember, and your instructor will help you.

Signs representing the following concepts are reviewed in this video segment:

1. REMOTE-CONTROL
2. CHAIR
3. COUCH
4. LIVING+ROOM
5. TV
6. ON
7. UNDER
8. BEHIND
9. IN
10. BED+ROOM
11. BED
12. DRESSER
13. UPSTAIRS
14. OVEN
15. REFRIGERATOR
16. SINK
17. TTY/TDD
18. TELEPHONE
19. LIGHT
20. FLASHING-LIGHT
21. BATH

5.19 Video Learning Experience

Lesson Three Review: Sentences

Viewing Goal: To improve your comprehension skills by watching sentences presented in ASL.

Viewing Instructions: Watch the signed sentences for comprehension. Remember to watch the face of each signer to see the facial/body expressions and the non-manual grammatical markers as well as the signs.

It is recommended that you copy each signed sentence when it is repeated.

In the space below, record any questions or notes you have regarding the sentences.

_____

_____

_____

_____

_____

_____

5.20 Video Learning Experience

Lesson Three Review: Practice Dialogue

Viewing Goal: To improve your comprehension skills by watching a dialogue presented in ASL.

Viewing Instructions: Watch the signed dialogue for comprehension and write a summary.

_____

_____

_____

_____

_____

5.21 Experiential Activity

Dynamic-Duo Dialogue

Activity Goal: To improve your expressive and receptive ASL skills.

Activity Instructions: Work with a partner to create a dialogue using the Lesson Three vocabulary (see the Sign Illustration Section for Lesson Three vocabulary). Use ASL (no voices needed!) and be sure each person takes at least four turns. Be prepared to share your dialogue with the class!

_____

_____

_____

_____

5.22 Video Learning Experience

Bravo Family Revisited

Viewing Goal: To reinforce your ASL expressive and receptive skills by reviewing a Bravo family interaction from Lesson Three.

Viewing Instructions: Watch the *Bravo Family Revisited* for review. Be prepared to use ASL to summarize what happened in this video segment!

_____

_____

_____

_____

5.23
Experiential
Activity

Point and Sign

Activity Goal: To improve your skills with the ASL vocabulary learned in Lesson Four.

Activity Instructions: Using the pictures below, follow your teacher's instructions to practice your signing skills.

5.24 Video Learning Experience

Lesson Four Review: Vocabulary

Viewing Goal: To help you review the ASL vocabulary from Lesson Four.

Viewing Instructions: Watch the Lesson Four vocabulary review.

Signs representing the following concepts are reviewed in this video segment:

1. SODA-POP	14. CHEESE	27. CANDY
2. ALL-GONE	15. HOT-DOG	28. COOKIES
3. FOOD	16. HAMBURGER	29. ICE-CREAM
4. SHOPPING	17. TURKEY	30. ONE
5. BANANA	18. FISH	31. TWO
6. MELON	19. CHICKEN	32. THREE
7. PLANT	20. BREAD	33. FOUR
8. EGG+PLANT	21. POPCORN	34. FIVE
9. LETTUCE	22. KETCHUP	35. SIX
10. ONION	23. SOUP	36. SEVEN
11. CARROT	24. TOMATO	37. EIGHT
12. COW	25. DOG+ FOOD	38. NINE
13. MILK	26. LOBSTER	39. TEN

5.25 Video Learning Experience

Lesson Four Review: Sentences

Viewing Goal: To improve your comprehension skills by watching sentences presented in ASL.

Viewing Instructions: Watch the signed sentences for comprehension. Remember to watch the face of each signer to see the facial/body expressions and the non-manual grammatical markers as well as the signs.

It is recommended that you copy each signed sentence when it is repeated.

In the space below, record any questions or notes you have regarding the sentences.

_____

_____

_____

_____

_____

_____

_____

5.26 Video Learning Experience

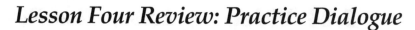

LESSON FIVE

Lesson Four Review: Practice Dialogue

Viewing Goal: To improve your comprehension skills by watching a dialogue presented in ASL.

Viewing Instructions: Watch the signed dialogue for comprehension and write a summary.

_____

_____

_____

_____

_____

_____

_____

_____

_____

5.27 Experiential Activity

Dynamic-Duo Dialogue

Activity Goal: To improve your expressive and receptive ASL skills.

Activity Instructions: Work with a partner to create a dialogue using Lesson Four vocabulary (see the Sign Illustration Section for Lesson Four vocabulary). Use ASL (no voices needed!) and be sure each person takes at least four turns.

Be prepared to share your dialogue with the class!

In the space below, record any ideas or notes you have regarding the dialogue.

_____

_____

_____

_____

_____

_____

_____

_____

_____

LESSON FIVE

5.28 Video Learning Experience

Bravo Family Revisited

Viewing Goal: To reinforce your ASL comprehension skills by watching a Bravo family interaction from Lesson Four.

Viewing Instructions: Watch the *Bravo Family Revisited* for review. In the space below, take notes or write a summary of the main points.

_____

_____

_____

_____

_____

_____

_____

5.29 Experiential Activity

Pictures in the Air

Activity Goal: To improve your expressive and comprehension skills.

Activity Instructions: Your instructor will divide the class into four groups and assign each group one of the pictures below.

Based on your picture, work with your group to create a skit using ASL. Your group will have time to prepare and practice your skit and then show it to the whole class.

5.30 Video Learning Experience

LESSON FIVE

Lessons One Thru Four Review: Cultural Notes A Cultural Challenge

Viewing Goal: To help you review the cultural aspects of ASL presented in Lessons One, Two, Three, and Four.

Viewing Instructions: Answer the questions below to see how well you remember these cultural aspects of ASL. When you are finished, watch the video. Billy will provide the answers so you can correct your work.

1. What three things do all cultures of the world have in common?

   _____

   _____

   _____

2. Name three culturally-appropriate ways to get a Deaf person's attention.

   _____

   _____

   _____

3. Name two commonly held perspectives of Deaf people.

   _____

   _____

   _____

4. Name three ways a Deaf person's home might be altered to become visually oriented.

   _____

   _____

   _____

5.31 Video Learning Experience

Number Story: The Bug

Viewing Goal: To enjoy a part of Deaf folklore by watching and practicing a signed Number Story.

Viewing Instructions: You will see a Number Story performed. Watch the story carefully, taking note of how each number is used.

When you have finished viewing *The Bug*, practice signing it with your partner. Help each other sign the story the way it was done on the video. Remember, facial expression is an important part of the story!

5.32 Video Learning Experience

Lessons One Thru Four Review: *Grammatical Notes* *A Grammatical Challenge*

Viewing Goal: To help you apply the grammatical aspects of ASL presented in Lessons One through Four.

Viewing Instructions: Watch Billy review the grammatical information taught in Lessons One through Four.

---

1. You will see three questions signed. Decide if these questions are all yes/no or wh-questions. Circle your answer.
   yes/no   wh

2. What are the non-manual markers that identify a wh-question?
   A. _____
   B. _____

3. Billy will show you three examples. You decide which are yes/no and which are wh-questions.
   1. yes/no   wh
   2. yes/no   wh
   3. yes/no   wh

4. Now you will see three sentences using topic/comment structure. Write the topic and comment for each sentence.

Topic	**Comment**
1. _____	_____
2. _____	_____
3. _____	_____

5.33 Video Learning Experience

LESSON FIVE

Lessons One Thru Four Review: *Practice Story*

Viewing Goal: To improve your ASL comprehension skills by watching a story presented in ASL.

Viewing Instructions: Watch the signed story for comprehension and write a summary of the main points.

_____

_____

_____

_____

_____

_____

_____

_____

_____

_____

5.34 Homework Assignment

Create-A-Story

Homework Goal: To improve your expressive ASL skills.

Homework Instructions: Create a story using one of the topics below. Be prepared to demonstrate your ASL story to the class!

A. You won't believe what happened when I woke up!

B. A funny thing happened at the food store!

C. You think your family is weird...

D. The breakfast of champions!

E. I found my dog in the most amazing place!

5.35 Post-test Introduction

What Do You Know Now?

Post-test Goal: To assess your mastery of the lesson objectives.

Post-test Introduction: This test has three sections:

Section One: The Comprehension section tests your ability to understand ASL.

Section Two: The Culture and Grammar section tests your knowledge of the material presented in the *Cultural* and *Grammatical Notes*.

Section Three: The Expressive portion tests your ability to use ASL.

Simply follow the instructions for each section.

Good luck!

Lesson 6
READ ANY GOOD FINGERS LATELY?

6.2 Homework Review

Create-A-Story

Activity Goal: To show the results of your homework assignment.

Activity Instructions: In small groups, take turns demonstrating the story you practiced for your homework assignment. You may use the sign illustrations in your workbooks for reference.

Remember you were to choose one of the following topics:

A. You won't believe what happened when I woke up!
B. A funny thing happened at the food store!
C. You think your family is weird…
D. The breakfast of champions!
E. I found my dog in the most amazing place!

Be creative! Ask each other questions in ASL about the topic of the story.

6.3 Pretest

What Do You Know?

Pretest Goal: To see how much you already know about what will be taught in this lesson.

Pretest Instructions: Read each question and circle the best answer.

1. Since Deaf people have complete mobility (they can walk), "access" is never a problem.
   A. True
   B. False

2. If you do not sign when a Deaf person is present, that person is likely to feel excluded.
   A. True
   B. False

3. When there are Deaf children in a family, it is especially important for the entire family to sign at all times.
   A. True
   B. False

4. Every sign has four parts. These parts are called:
   A. Hand-parts
   B. Sign-parts
   C. Parameters
   D. Paragrammars

5. Every sign is made of what four parts?
   A. Slow, medium, intermediate, and fast movements
   B. Fingers, waving, flipping, and flashing movements
   C. Circular, perpendicular, horizontal, and vertical movements
   D. Handshape, movement, location, and palm orientation

6. A sign produced accurately, but with the wrong movement, can change the meaning completely.
   A. True
   B. False

7. The manual alphabet is also referred to as "fingerspelling."
   A. True
   B. False

8. There are two sets of manual alphabets, one for capital letters and one for lower case letters.
   A. True
   B. False

9. Fingerspelling is used for proper names that don't have established signs.
   A. True
   B. False

10. If you are with a hearing friend and you see a Deaf person enter the room, you should start to sign even if your hearing friend doesn't understand Sign Language.
    A. True
    B. False

6.4 Lesson Objectives

Planning for Success

Goal: To see what you will learn by the end of this lesson.

Instructions: Read the objectives below.

Upon completing this VideoCourse lesson, you will be able to...

1. Recognize and accurately produce the ASL vocabulary introduced in this and all previous lessons.

2. Explain the importance of equal access and inclusion of Deaf people in all communication events.

3. Define and demonstrate the four parameters of sign production.

4. Correctly identify and accurately produce all 26 handshapes that represent the letters of the American manual alphabet.

5. Understand when and how fingerspelling is used within the context of signed communication.

6.5 Lesson Focus

Color Time

Activity Goal: To experience an activity with "colorful" signs!

Activity Instructions: Watch the signed instructions to see what colors to use for the objects in the pictures below. If you do not understand the signs, try to guess which colors to use.

6.6 Video Learning Experience

LESSON SIX

Bravo Family Visit

Viewing Goal: To get information about inclusion from watching a Bravo family interaction.

Viewing Instructions: Watch the Bravo family as they meet a school teacher at the food store. In the space below, write a summary of the main points.

_____

_____

_____

_____

_____

_____

Thought/Discussion Questions

1. Have you ever been in a situation where you didn't understand the language being spoken? If so, how did you feel?

_____

_____

_____

2. What are some situations in which Deaf people might still be excluded from full access? (How might access be improved for TV programs, movies, radio programming, airport communication, restaurants, paging systems, religious ceremonies, etc.?)

_____

_____

_____

3. What are things you could do to help increase access for Deaf people?

_____

_____

_____

LESSON SIX

6.7 Experiential Activity

Read My Lips

Activity Goal: To show you a lecture to help you learn.

Activity Instructions: Watch the video very carefully. There will be a quiz immediately following this segment.

Quiz:

1. What was the main topic of this talk?

   _____

2. The term speech-reading is also called

   _____.

3. The ability to lip-read is directly linked to a how smart a person is.

   A. True
   B. False

4. A person who lip-reads also gets a lot of information from _____.

5. According to the speaker, what percentage of the English language can be seen on the lips?

   _____

Thought/Discussion Questions

1. How did you do on the quiz when the program was not accessible?

   _____

   _____

2. How would you do in school if you had to depend on lipreading?

   _____

   _____

3. What are some adjectives to describe how you felt while viewing the tape?

   _____

   _____

---

4. How would you deal with a lifetime of these kinds of experiences?

_____

_____

_____

5. How did you feel about using the captions for access to this program?

_____

_____

_____

6. What did you learn from this experience?

_____

_____

_____

6.8 Language Learning Instruction

Learning New Signs

Goal: To help you learn new ASL vocabulary.

Instructions: Your instructor will teach you new signs! Watch closely to learn what these signs mean and how they are produced.

In the space below, record any notes to help you remember the signs.

_____

_____

_____

_____

_____

_____

_____

_____

_____

6.9 Video Learning Experience

Introduction to New Vocabulary

Viewing Goal: To help you learn new ASL vocabulary.

Viewing Instructions: Watch how Billy produces each sign. Be sure to notice the facial/body expressions. Copy the signs as Billy repeats each one.

Signs representing the following concepts are introduced:

1. ORANGE
2. BLUE
3. GREEN
4. RED
5. YELLOW
6. PURPLE
7. WHITE
8. BROWN
9. SILVER
10. GOLD
11. PINK
12. BLACK
13. TAN

6.10 Video Learning Experience

Bravo Family Visit

Viewing Goal: To improve your ASL comprehension skills by watching a Bravo family interaction.

Viewing Instructions: Watch the signed interaction and write a summary of the main points.

_____

_____

_____

_____

_____

_____

_____

6.11 Experiential Activity

Color Time Again!

Activity Goal: To assist you in recognizing new vocabulary.

Activity Instructions: Look at the pictures below. Use colored pens or crayons to color the objects in the picture following the signed directions.

6.12 Language Learning Instruction

Learning Fingerspelling

Goal: To help you learn to recognize fingerspelling.

Instructions: Your instructor will show you how to fingerspell names. Watch carefully to learn how to recognize your name and your classmates' names!

In the space below, record any notes to help you remember.

_____

_____

_____

_____

_____

_____

_____

_____

_____

_____

6.13 Video Learning Experience

LESSON SIX

Introduction to Fingerspelling

Viewing Goal: To help you learn each letter of the manual alphabet (fingerspelling).

Viewing Instructions: Watch the video carefully to see how Billy produces each fingerspelled letter.

Fingerspelled letters representing each letter of the alphabet are introduced in this video segment.

A B C D E F G H I J K L M
N O P Q R S T U V W X Y Z

Hint: This great practice sentence contains every letter in the alphabet! See if you can fingerspell the whole sentence...

"The quick brown fox jumped over the lazy dogs."

6.14 Video Learning Experience

LESSON SIX

Practice Session: Fingerspelling

Viewing Goal: To produce each of the fingerspelled letters correctly.

Viewing Instructions: Watch how Billy produces each fingerspelled letter. The video will show you how each letter should look from both your perspective as well as the person to whom you are fingerspelling. Copy the handshapes as Billy signs each one.

6.15 Experiential Activity

SIGN-O

Activity Goal: To practice comprehension of colors and fingerspelling.

Activity Instructions: The class will play SIGN-O (just like the game BINGO). Use the SIGN-O card below.

Follow your instructor's signed directions and use markers or crayons to color the shapes on the top of the card.

Write the letters of the alphabet in random order (not in alphabetical order) in the blank squares on the card.

Your instructor will sign a color and then a letter. For example, BLUE - F. If this color/letter combination is on your card, place a coin, chip, scrap of paper or an "X" with a pencil (so you can use the card again) on the appropriate square.

When you have an entire row marked, you should stand up and fingerspell S-I-G-N-O.

Good luck and have fun!

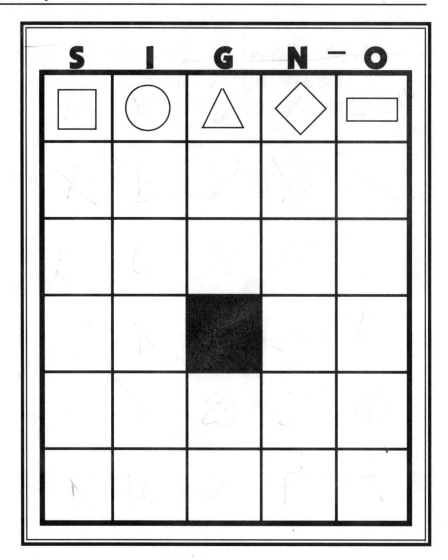

6.16 Video Learning Experience

Practice Session: Fingerspelling Usage

Viewing Goal: To learn when to use fingerspelling and practice forming words.

Viewing Instructions: There are specific times when you should fingerspell words. There are also specific rules for fingerspelling. The following is an outline of what Billy teaches about the use of fingerspelling. Please review the information on the following page.

LESSON SIX

I. When is fingerspelling used?

  A. For a person's name.

  B. For the name of a place.

  C. For things for which there is no established sign.

II. Rules regarding fingerspelling:

  A. Fingerspell smoothly (go from one letter to the next without extra movements).

  B. Keep the movement going (avoid stopping after each letter).

  C. Keep hand steady (do not bounce your hand with each letter).

  D. When you are reading fingerspelling, sound the word out the way you do when you are reading a book (do not say each letter as it is signed).

  E. When fingerspelling, look at the person to whom you are signing (rather than looking at your hand).

6.17A
Experiential Activity

Fingercise #1

Activity Goal: To learn how to read fingerspelling by watching for the shape of words that are fingerspelled instead of trying to see each individual letter.

Activity Instructions: Fill in the blank boxes below with the correct letters. Think about the shape of the whole word as well as the category to which the word belongs.

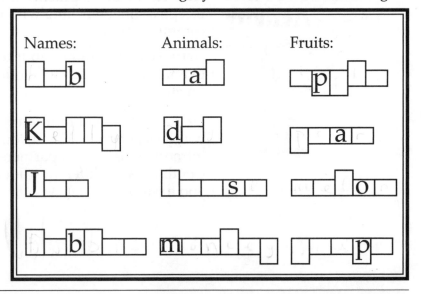

Names: Animals: Fruits:

6.17B Experiential Activity

Fingercise #2

Activity Goal: To improve receptive fingerspelling skills.

Activity Instructions: Fill in the blanks below with the correct letters. This activity will help you see that you can miss several letters in a fingerspelled word and still be able to figure out what is being fingerspelled.

I w _ n _   to   g _   _ o   th _   s _ _ _ _.

Wh _   a _ e   y _ _   l _ _ k _ _ g   at   _ e?

D _   y _ _   l _ v _   S _ _ _   L _ _ _ _ _ _ _ e?

H _ _   o _ _   ar _   y _ _?

F _ ng _ _ _ _ _ l _ _ _ g   c _ _   be   f _ _!!

6.17C Experiential Activity

Fingercise #3

Activity Goal: To practice the use of expressive and receptive fingerspelling within the context of signed communication.

Activity Instructions: Your teacher will show you how to introduce yourself to another person using signs and fingerspelling.

Find a partner and introduce yourself the way you saw your teacher do it. When you have both finished your introductions, switch partners and practice again. Continue with different students until your teacher tells you to stop.

6.18 Video Learning Experience

LESSON SIX

ABC Story

Viewing Goal: To learn about ABC Stories as a part of Deaf folklore.

Viewing Instructions: Watch as Billy introduces an original ABC Story. Notice how the handshapes used in the story follow the manual alphabet. Be sure to notice how Billy uses the handshapes with facial/body expression to create the story! You may want to copy Billy as he signs the story!

_____

_____

_____

_____

_____

_____

_____

_____

_____

_____

6.19 Experiential Activity

Simple as A, B, C!

Activity Goal: To participate in creating an ABC Story.

Activity Instructions: You and your classmates will create an ABC Story similar to the one Billy showed you on the video.

Be creative, but remember to only use the handshapes of the alphabet!

Don't worry, if you get stuck, your teacher will help you. When the story is complete, you will be given a chance to practice signing the story.

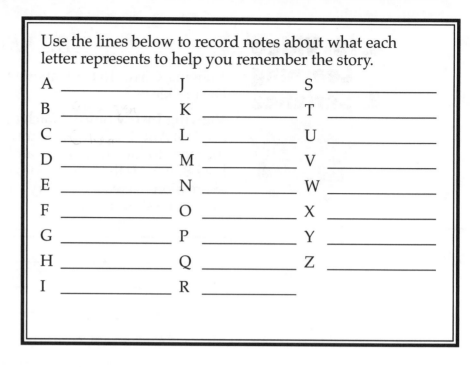

Use the lines below to record notes about what each letter represents to help you remember the story.

A _____ J _____ S _____

B _____ K _____ T _____

C _____ L _____ U _____

D _____ M _____ V _____

E _____ N _____ W _____

F _____ O _____ X _____

G _____ P _____ Y _____

H _____ Q _____ Z _____

I _____ R _____

6.20 Video Learning Experience

Cultural Notes

Viewing Goal: To learn about the cultural aspects of ASL.

Viewing Instructions: View the *Cultural Notes* segment carefully for the following:

Inclusion and accessibility:

A. Example given: The art teacher who met the Bravo family at the food store learned about the importance of using Sign Language when Deaf people (such as the members of the Bravo family) are present so that they may feel included.

B. Viewers are encouraged to sign whenever there is a Deaf person present.

C. Billy shared the importance of signing at all times when there are Deaf children in a family. This provides the children with an opportunity to participate and to know they are important and valued members of the family.

6.21A Experiential Activity

Access to Another Culture!

Activity Goal: To learn cultural information from a person who comes from a different country.

Activity Instructions: Watch the video of a speaker from another country and use the space below to take notes:

_____

_____

_____

_____

_____

_____

_____

_____

Thought/Discussion Questions: Part A

1. Were you interested in what this person was saying?

   _____

2. Could you figure out some of the information?

   _____

3. What are some adjectives to describe how you felt during this experience?

   _____

4. Do you think this is similar to how Deaf people might feel sometimes?

   _____

5. How could this information be made accessible to you?

   _____

6. Would you like to view this segment again, with captions or an interpreter?

   _____

6.21B Experiential Activity

Access to Another Culture!

Activity Goal: To gain access to the speaker from another country with the use of an interpreter or captions.

Activity Instructions: You will view the speaker from another country again. This time, you will have access to the information through an interpreter and/or captions. Use the space below to take notes:

_____

_____

_____

_____

Thought/Discussion Questions: Part B

1. How did the interpreter and/or captions change this experience for you?

_____

_____

2. What are some adjectives to describe how you felt while you were viewing the interpreted/captioned version?

_____

_____

3. Do you think this is similar to how Deaf people feel when they are using interpreters?

_____

_____

_____

4. Do you think society provides adequate access for Deaf people?

_____

6.22 Video Learning Experience

LESSON SIX

Grammatical Notes

Viewing Goal: To learn some of the grammatical aspects of ASL.

Viewing Instructions: View the *Grammatical Notes* segment carefully for the following:

I. The four parts - or parameters - of every sign include:
   A. Handshape
   B. Movement
   C. Location/Position
   D. Palm orientation

II. Example: The four parameters of the sign YELLOW are:
   A. The handshape is a "Y."
   B. The movement demonstrated shows a side-to-side, wrist twisting movement.
   C. The position/location demonstrated is at the front of body on the dominant hand side.
   D. Palm orientation is facing to the side opposite the dominant hand.

III. Billy's recommendation: As you view the video, observe each of the four parameters for all the new vocabulary to ensure accurate production.

6.23 Experiential Activity

What Sign Am I Thinking Of?

Activity Goal: To have the opportunity to practice using the four parameters of sign production.

Activity Instructions: Your teacher will divide the class into pairs. Student "A" will go first. "A" will select a vocabulary item from this or any previous lesson and describe each of the four parameters of that sign to student "B."

"B" should follow the parameters being described and begin to produce the sign until "B" can guess and correctly produce the sign that "A" described.

Switch roles and repeat this exercise several times.

6.24 Video Learning Experience

Practice Session: Sentences

Viewing Goal: To improve your comprehension skills by watching sentences presented in ASL.

Viewing Instructions: Watch the signed sentences for comprehension. Remember to watch the face of each signer to see the facial/body expressions and the non-manual grammatical markers as well as the signs.

It is recommended that you copy each signed sentence when it is repeated.

In the space below, record any questions or notes you have regarding the sentences.

_____

_____

_____

_____

_____

_____

_____

_____

6.25 Video Learning Experience

Practice Session: Story

Viewing Goal: To improve your comprehension by watching a story presented in ASL.

Viewing Instructions: Watch the signed story for comprehension. In the space below, write a summary of the main points to help you remember the story.

_____

_____

_____

_____

_____

_____

_____

_____

6.26 Comprehension Quiz

What Did You Understand?

Quiz Goal: To see how much of the signed story you understood.

Quiz Instructions: Your instructor will play the practice story again. Watch carefully and color the items in the picture below with the colors Billy describes in the story. If you don't have colored crayons or markers, write the name of the correct color on each item.

Not
Green
White
Black
Braun

6.27 Homework Assignment

Come Home With Me!

Homework Goal: To practice using the new vocabulary and fingerspelling in a story.

Homework Instructions: Create a short story about your home. Be sure to include who lives there (fingerspell all the names) and describe all the rooms, including room color and contents. 5 Signs from ch. 6 (colors)
3 Spelled Names (fingers)

_____

_____

_____

_____

6.28 Post-test Introduction

What Do You Know Now?

Post-test Goal: To assess your mastery of the lesson objectives.

Post-test Introduction: This test has three sections:

Section One: The Comprehension section tests your ability to understand ASL.

Section Two: The Culture and Grammar section tests your knowledge of the material presented in the *Cultural* and *Grammatical Notes*.

Section Three: The Expressive portion tests your ability to use ASL.

Simply follow the instructions for each section.

Good luck!

Lesson 7
A School 'Daze'

7.2 Homework Review

Come Home With Me!

Activity Goal: To show the results of your homework assignment.

Activity Instructions: In your small group, take turns signing the story about your home that you practiced for your homework assignment.

Remember to include the fingerspelled names of all the people who live in your home and a description of the rooms (including room color and contents).

Be creative! Ask questions about each other's homes using ASL.

7.3 Pretest

What Do You Know?

Pretest Goal: To see how much you already know about what will be taught in this lesson.

Pretest Instructions: Read and answer each question.

1. All Deaf children attend schools for the Deaf.
   - A. True
   - B. False

2. In order for a Deaf child to attend a school for the Deaf, s/he must live away from home.
   - A. True
   - B. False

3. The self-esteem and self-identity of a Deaf child is an important factor when making educational decisions.
   - A. True
   - B. False

4. In ASL, the movement of a sign often gives vital information.

   A. True
   B. False

5. In ASL, the meaning of a sign can be changed by simply changing the movement of the sign.

   A. True
   B. False

7.4 Lesson Objectives

Planning For Success

Goal: To see what you will learn by the end of this lesson.

Instructions: Read the objectives below.

Upon completing this VideoCourse lesson, you will be able to...

1. Recognize and accurately produce the ASL vocabulary introduced in this and all previous lessons.

2. Explain what directional verbs are and how they are used.

3. Demonstrate at least three verbs that are directional.

4. Explain the importance of schools for the Deaf.

5. Explain the importance of fostering strong self-esteem and self-identity in Deaf children.

6. Identify some of the basic educational options available to Deaf children.

7. Identify the criteria that must be considered when choosing the best educational option for each Deaf child.

7.5 Lesson Focus

Charades Race

Activity Goal: To play a game that will help you improve your skills.

Activity Instructions: Your instructor will divide your class into two teams. Each team will send one person to the front of the classroom. These two players will face their teams while your instructor stands behind them and writes a word on the board.

Use gestures and mime to help your team player guess the word. The team that gets their player to write the correct word on the board first receives a point. Remember, you are not allowed to use your voice or written words.

Have fun and good luck!

7.6 Language Learning Instruction

Learning New Signs

Goal: To help you learn new ASL vocabulary.

Instructions: Your instructor will teach you new signs! Watch closely to learn what these signs mean and how they are produced.

In the space below, record any notes to help you remember the signs.

_____

_____

_____

_____

_____

_____

_____

_____

_____

_____

LESSON SEVEN

7.7 Video Learning Experience

Introduction to New Vocabulary

Viewing Goal: To help you learn new ASL vocabulary.

Viewing Instructions: Watch how Billy produces each sign. Be sure to notice the facial/body expressions. Copy the signs as Billy repeats each one.

Signs representing the following concepts are introduced in this segment:

1. SCHOOL
2. TEACHER
3. BOOK
4. READ
5. SIT
6. TIRED
7. SORRY
8. FLOWER
9. PICK+FLOWER
10. HERE
11. THERE
12. GROW-UP

7.8 Video Learning Experience

Bravo Family Visit

Viewing Goal: To improve your ASL comprehension skills by watching a Bravo family interaction.

Viewing Instructions: Watch the signed interaction and write a summary of the main points.

_____

_____

_____

_____

_____

_____

_____

_____

7.9 Comprehension Quiz

What Did You Understand?

Quiz Goal: To see how much of the Bravo family interaction you understood.

Quiz Instructions: Read and answer each question below.

1. Scott and Anna are both ready to go to school.
   A. True
   B. False

2. The gardener invites Anna to pick a beautiful flower at her school.
   A. True
   B. False

3. The book Anna wants is only for _____.
   A. Students
   B. Mothers
   C. Teachers
   D. Children

4. Once in class, Anna is told by the teacher that she is in the wrong chair.
   A. True
   B. False

5. Anna decides to leave school for the day so nobody will tell her "No!"
   A. True
   B. False

7.10 Language Learning Instruction

Learning New Signs

Goal: To help you learn new ASL vocabulary.

Instructions: Your instructor will teach you new signs! Watch closely to learn what these signs mean and how they are produced.

In the space below, record any notes to help you remember the signs.

_____

_____

_____

_____

_____

_____

_____

_____

_____

_____

_____

7.11 Video Learning Experience

LESSON SEVEN

Introduction to New Vocabulary

Viewing Goal: To help you learn new ASL vocabulary.

Viewing Instructions: Watch how Billy produces each sign. Be sure to notice the facial/body expressions. Copy the signs as Billy repeats each one.

Signs representing the following concepts are introduced in this video segment:

1. TEACH	7. WHAT-WRONG	13. NEED
2. LEARN	8. NOT	14. PLEASE
3. STUDENT	9. WHO	15. HAVE
4. STUDY	10. PENCIL	16. WANT
5. GIVE	11. PAPER	17. LATE
6. PLAY	12. GOOD	18. FINISH

**7.12
Experiential
Activity**

Point and Sign

Activity Goal: To improve your ASL receptive and expressive skills.

Activity Instructions: Using the pictures below, follow your teacher's instructions and practice using your new ASL vocabulary.

7.13 Experiential Activity

Crossword Puzzle

Activity Goal: To help you recognize the ASL vocabulary learned in this lesson.

Activity Instructions: You will see several of your new ASL vocabulary items signed with a reference as to where you should write them on the puzzle. For example, the signer might tell you... "One Across - SCHOOL."

Write the English word that fits in the puzzle and describes what is being signed in the correct boxes. Each item will be presented twice.

7.14 Video Learning Experience

Bravo Family Visit

Viewing Goal: To improve your ASL comprehension skills by watching a Bravo family interaction.

Viewing Instructions: Watch the signed interaction and write a summary of the main points.

_____

_____

_____

_____

_____

_____

_____

_____

7.15 Comprehension Quiz

What Did You Understand?

Quiz Goal: To see how much of the Bravo family interaction you understood.

Quiz Instructions: Read and answer each question

1. The first student in Anna's class comes in feeling _____.
   A. Sick
   B. Tired
   C. Happy
   D. Hungry

2. The student who was late doesn't like school.
   A. True
   (B) False

3. The student who was late told Anna that she was _____.
   A. Tired
   (B.) Sorry
   C. Good
   D. Playing

LESSON SEVEN

4. Anna asks her students to get their _____ ready.

   A. Books
   B. Flowers
   C. Paper and pencils
   D. Paper and crayons

5. Two students argue over a book. This book belongs to _____.

   A. Mom
   B. Dad
   C. The teacher
   D. The library

7.16 Video Learning Experience

Grammatical Notes

Viewing Goal: To learn about the grammatical aspects of ASL.

Viewing Instructions: View the *Grammatical Notes* segment carefully for the following:

Some verbs in ASL are called "directional verbs."

A. The movement of directional verbs gives important information about who is doing or receiving an action. For example, HELP-ME can become HELP-YOU or HELP-HIM/HER simply by changing the direction of the sign's movement.

B. Example from the video: The kids fighting over the book...

GIVE-ME

GIVE-HIM, NOT

GIVE-ME, ME-GIVE-HER

C. You can change the meaning of WRITE:

WRITE-PAPER

WRITE-BOARD

WRITE-BACK+FORTH

D. Other examples:

JOIN

WATCH

7.17 Experiential Activity

question ?

help her
help me

pay

It's Your Move

Activity Goal: To practice using directional verbs.

Activity Instructions: You have just learned about different meanings that a sign might have, depending on the directionality of the sign. HELP, for example, can be signed in one direction for "I'll help you," and in a different direction for "You help me."

With a partner, practice signing different sentences using some of the examples in this video lesson.
Remember that you need to change the movement/directionality in order to change the meaning.

Create sentences using the following directional verbs:

HELP	GIVE	READ
WRITE	WATCH	TEACH

Fool me

join
tell

7.18 Video Learning Experience

Bravo Family Visit

Viewing Goal: To improve your ASL comprehension skills by watching a Bravo family interaction.

Viewing Instructions: Watch the signed interaction and write a summary of the main points to help you remember the interaction.

_____

_____

_____

_____

_____

_____

_____

LESSON SEVEN

7.19 Video Learning Experience

LESSON SEVEN

Review Session

Viewing Goal: To help you remember how to produce the signs introduced in this lesson.

Viewing Instructions: Watch this video segment carefully to see how each sign is made, and note any hints that might help you remember. You may want to copy the signs as you watch Billy.

Following are the vocabulary items and explanations offered in this video segment:

TEACH	The information from one person's head is given to another person.
TEACHER	This sign indicates a person who teaches.
LEARN	You take the information from a book and put it in your mind.
STUDENT	This is similar to the sign for TEACHER, as it indicates a person who is learning.
SCHOOL	When a teacher wants to get the students' attention, s/he claps her/his hands.
BOOK	This sign indicates how a person opens a book.
READ	The index and middle fingers are the "eyes." The flat hand is a book. The "eyes" move along, reading the book.
STUDY	This follows the same idea as READ but now there are more fingers indicating eyes staring at the page or reading the page again and again.
SORRY	Someone's feelings (over the heart) have been hurt. Your face must reflect that you are SORRY.
FLOWER	The sign for FLOWER is placed around the nose because most flowers smell good.
PICK+FLOWER	This is an action sign that looks like picking a flower.
GIVE-TO-ME	This is another example of a directional verb. Perhaps something has been picked and given to me. Now, I can change the direction of the sign to show...ME-GIVE-HIM, HE-GIVE-ME, HE-GIVE-HER, etc.
PLAY	This sign represents the attitude of being relaxed and playful.

WHAT-WRONG	The sign for WRONG is used. But when we soften it, repeat the movement, and give a questioning look it becomes, WHAT-WRONG.
WHO	The old sign for WHO was this (shown on tape), but it has evolved into the present sign WHO.
PENCIL	Long ago, you had to moisten the lead to soften it so that you could write with it. That is the origin of the sign PENCIL.
PAPER	Paper was once manufactured in a very large machine which flattened it out and rolled it up.
WRITE	Remember the description of the sign for PENCIL? Well, this sign shows the action of WRITING.
NEED/MUST	This sign reflects the position of the body of a person who is saying you have to, you MUST.
HAVE	This shows that there is something you hold in your possession (toward your body).
WANT	There is something out there that I want, so I pull it to me.
DON'T-WANT	If I don't want something, I push it away.
LATE	When I'm late, I run to get there on time.
FINISH	It's like a rodeo. In steer roping, they lasso the steer, tie its legs, and raise their hands to say, FINISH!
PLEASE	This sign is made over the heart.
GROW-UP	This sign shows the top of the head raising as the child grows taller.
SIT	This sign follows the action of a person sitting down.
TIRED	The body droops when a person is TIRED.

good mouth to open hand

LESSON SEVEN

7.20 Experiential Activity

Signs and Origins

Activity Goal: To help you remember how to produce some of the new ASL vocabulary.

Activity Instructions: With a partner, use ASL to discuss the hints Billy gave you about each of the signs listed below (from the video Review Session). These hints will help you remember how to make each sign. You may take notes in the space below to help you remember.

Sign	Origin/visual hint
1. SCHOOL	_____
2. TEACHER	_____
3. BOOK	_____
4. FLOWER	_____
5. GROW-UP	_____
6. LEARN	_____
7. GIVE	_____
8. PAPER	_____
9. TIRED	_____
10. STUDY	_____

7.21 Video Learning Experience

LESSON SEVEN

Cultural Notes

Viewing Goal: To help you learn about the cultural aspects of ASL.

Viewing Instructions: View the *Cultural Notes* segment carefully for the following:

I. The topic of this segment is Deaf Education:

    A. The potential success of Deaf students (academic and personal) is dependent on teaching methods, the school the child attends, and the way the child learns.

    B. School-age children learn many things:

        1. Education is not limited to reading, writing, and arithmetic.

LESSON SEVEN

2. It is important for children to have the opportunity for self-discovery (finding out who they are, what they can do, and how they feel about themselves).

C. How can self-esteem and positive self-identity be addressed?

1. Historically, discussions regarding Deaf education often overlooked critical issues regarding self-esteem.

2. These issues impact how children relate to the world, set goals, and make decisions about their futures.

D. Schools must be accessible!

1. Focus on what the child **can** do.

2. Encourage capabilities.

3. Provide exciting possibilities for each child.

II. Educational options for Deaf children:

A. Schools for the Deaf options:

1. Residential school where students live at the school.

2. Day school where students live at home and commute.

Note: Deaf adults serve as role models in both options.

B. Mainstream program (with the use of interpreters):

1. A self-contained classroom typically has all Deaf students.

2. Deaf students are placed in classrooms with hearing students.

III. Making an educational decision:

A. An appropriate placement must consider the child's:

1. Skills

2. Capabilities

3. Motivation

4. Personal interests

B. Overall well-being must be a factor, including:

1. Mental and spiritual needs.

2. Opportunity for growth, learning, building self-pride, resources for learning about Deaf culture and ASL, and encouragement of self-discovery.

7.22 Cultural and Grammatical Quiz

What Did You Learn?

Quiz Goal: To see how much of this lesson's cultural and grammatical information you learned.

Quiz Instructions: Read and answer each question.

1. Self-esteem and self-identity are important factors in choosing a school for a Deaf child.

   A. True
   B. False

2. In order to get an education, Deaf children must live away from their families.

   A. True
   B. False

3. Having Deaf adult role models is one benefit of residential schools for the Deaf.

   A. True
   B. False

4. How can movement change an ASL sign? (Select all that apply.)

   A. Gives additional information
   B. Changes the meaning of the sign
   C. Changes the facial expression
   D. Changes who is doing the signing

5. Give two examples of ASL signs that are considered directional verbs.

   _____

   _____

6. If a Deaf student were to attend your school, what modifications (changes) would be needed so that student would gain full access to all educational activities? (Check all that apply.)

   A. Interpreters for classes
   B. Lights flashing for bells
   C. Captions or subtitles for DVDs and television
   D. Video phone (VP) or computer with camera for phone calls.

7.23 Video Learning Experience

LESSON SEVEN

Practice Session: Sentences

Viewing Goal: To improve your comprehension skills by watching sentences presented in ASL.

Viewing Instructions: Watch the signed sentences for comprehension. Remember to watch the face of each signer to see the facial/body expressions and the non-manual grammatical markers as well as the signs. It is recommended that you copy each signed sentence when it is repeated.

In the space below, record any questions or notes you have regarding the sentences.

_____

_____

_____

_____

_____

_____

_____

_____

_____

_____

7.24 Experiential Activity

Receptivity Race

Activity Goal: To improve your receptive and expressive ASL skills.

Activity Instructions: Your class will be divided into two teams. One player from each team will go to the front of the room. Your teacher will show each player a topic. The player is to sign several examples related to each topic to his/her team.

Watch closely and try to guess the topic! The team to guess the topic first wins a point. Take turns going to the front of the class to help your team win!

Good luck!

7.25 Video Learning Experience

Practice Session: Story

Viewing Goal: To improve your comprehension skills by watching a story presented in ASL.

Viewing Instructions: Watch the signed story for comprehension. In the space below, write a summary to help you remember the story.

_____

_____

_____

_____

_____

_____

_____

_____

_____

7.26 Comprehension Quiz

What Did You Understand?

Quiz Goal: To see how much of the signed story you understood.

Quiz Instructions: Read and answer each question.

1. The teacher in the story signed fluently.

   A. True
   B. False

2. The other children in the class were also Deaf.

   A. True
   B. False

3. How many members of the boy's family were Deaf?

   A. 1
   B. 2
   C. 3
   D. 5

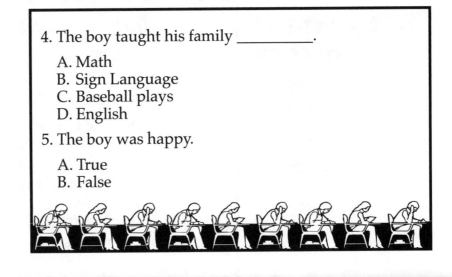

4. The boy taught his family _____.

   A. Math
   B. Sign Language
   C. Baseball plays
   D. English

5. The boy was happy.

   A. True
   B. False

7.27 Homework Assignment

A Funny Thing Happened At School

Activity Goal: To improve your expressive skills.

Activity Instructions: Prepare a signed story about a day at school. Use at least six of your new vocabulary signs and at least three directional verbs (as taught in the *Grammatical Notes* segment).

Be prepared to sign your story for the class.

7.28 Post-test Introduction

What Do You Know Now?

Post-test Goal: To assess your mastery of the lesson objectives.

Post-test Introduction: This test has three sections.

Section One: The Comprehension section tests your ability to understand ASL.

Section Two: Culture and Grammar section tests your knowledge of the material presented in the *Cultural* and *Grammatical Notes.*

Section Three: Expressive portion tests your ability to use ASL.

Simply follow the instructions for each section.

Good luck!

Lesson 8
A School 'Daze' - The Sequel

8.2 Homework Review

A Funny Thing Happened At School

Activity Goal: To show the results of your homework assignment.

Activity Instructions: In small groups, take turns signing the story about a day at school that you practiced for your homework assignment.

Remember to include at least six new school-related signs and three directional verbs. Be creative! Ask questions about each other's stories using ASL.

8.3 Pretest

What Do You Know?

Pretest Goal: To see how much you already know about what will be taught in this lesson.

Pretest Instructions: Read each question and circle the best answer.

1. One benefit of a residential school for the Deaf is that all of the students are Deaf.

   A. True
   B. False

2. The first school for the Deaf established in America was the _____.

   A. Model School for the Deaf
   B. United States School for the Deaf
   C. American School for the Deaf
   D. Hartford School for the Deaf

3. What year was the first school for the Deaf established?

A. 1955
B. 1857
C. 1917
D. 1817

4. Members of the Deaf community often view the local school for the Deaf as:

A. A place that helps and supports Deaf people.
B. Providing a strong sense of belonging.
C. A place with warm childhood memories.
D. All of the above

5. In ASL, a simple side-to-side headshake can turn a positive statement into a negative.

A. True
B. False

8.4 Lesson Objectives

Planning for Success

Goal: To see what you will learn by the end of this lesson.

Instructions: Read the objectives below.

Upon completing this VideoCourse lesson, you will be able to...

1. Recognize and accurately produce the vocabulary introduced in this and all previous lessons.

2. Summarize the benefits of attending a residential school for the Deaf.

3. Explain the history and importance of the American School for the Deaf.

4. Explain the Deaf community's view of residential schools for the Deaf.

5. When formulating signed sentences, choose conceptually accurate signs that are based on meaning.

LESSON EIGHT

8.5 Lesson Focus

Math Whiz Quiz

Activity Goal: To solve math problems presented in ASL.

Activity Instructions: You will see ten signed math problems. Solve each problem and circle the correct answer below. If you don't know the signed numbers, try your best guess!

Don't worry - after this lesson you will know the ASL numbers you need to solve these problems!

1. A. 2
   B. 3
   C. 5
   D. 1

2. A. 23
   B. 13
   C. 16
   D. 3

3. A. 0
   B. 11
   C. 16
   D. 7

4. A. 4
   B. 10
   C. 6
   D. 1

5. A. 23
   B. 7
   C. 5
   D. 26

6. A. 10
   B. 11
   C. 30
   D. 9

7. A. 19
   B. 10
   C. 20
   D. 4

8. A. 4
   B. 17
   C. 2
   D. 5

9. A. 19
   B. 18
   C. 17
   D. 2

10. A. 14
    B. 8
    C. 6
    D. 18

Thought/Discussion Questions

1. What are some signed numbers that would have been useful to know during this activity?

_____

_____

_____

2. How did it feel to be limited in your ability to understand the problems?

_____

_____

_____

3. Do you think Deaf people ever feel that way?

_____

_____

_____

8.6 Video Learning Experience

LESSON EIGHT

Bravo Family Visit

Viewing Goal: To help you remember Anna's dream at the School for the Deaf from Lesson Seven.

Viewing Instructions: Watch the review of what happened at the School for the Deaf. In the space below, write a summary of the main points.

_____

_____

_____

_____

_____

_____

_____

_____

8.7 Language Learning Instruction

Learning New Signs

Goal: To help you learn the numbers 11-20.

Instructions: Your instructor will teach you new signs! Watch closely to learn what these signs mean and how they are produced.

In the space below, record any notes to help you remember the signs.

_____

_____

_____

_____

_____

_____

_____

_____

8.8 Video Learning Experience

Practice Session: Numbers

Viewing Goal: To review numbers 1-10 and learn numbers 11-20.

Viewing Instructions: Watch how Billy produces the numbers.

In the space below, record any notes that will help you remember these numbers.

1. #1	6. #6	11. #11	16. #16
2. #2	7. #7	12. #12	17. #17
3. #3	8. #8	13. #13	18. #18
4. #4	9. #9	14. #14	19. #19
5. #5	10. #10	15. #15	20. #20

_____

_____

_____

_____

_____

LESSON EIGHT

8.9 Language Learning Instruction

Learning New Signs

Goal: To help you learn new ASL signs.

Instructions: Your instructor will teach you new signs! Watch closely to learn what these signs mean and how they are produced.

In the space below, record any notes that will help you remember the signs.

_____

_____

_____

_____

_____

_____

_____

_____

_____

_____

8.10 Video Learning Experience

Introduction to New Vocabulary

Viewing Goal: To help you learn new ASL vocabulary.

Viewing Instructions: Watch how Billy produces each sign. Be sure to notice the facial/body expressions. Copy the signs as Billy repeats each one.

Signs representing the following concepts are introduced:

1. MATH
2. PLUS
3. MINUS/NEGATIVE
4. EQUAL
5. RIGHT/CORRECT
6. WRONG/INCORRECT
7. KNOW
8. CALCULATOR
9. COUNT
10. COME
11. ADD
12. TOGETHER
13. UNDERSTAND

8.11 Experiential Activity

Fish, Go You!

Activity Goal: To improve your expressive and receptive skills with numbers.

Activity Instructions: Your instructor will divide you into groups to play a version of the game "Go Fish." We call our game "FISH, GO YOU!" (following ASL topic/comment sentence structure).

The dealer gives each player six cards, face down. The remaining cards should be placed in a pile face down in the center of the group. The goal is to find a match for each card by asking another player, in ASL, if s/he has the card you need.

When it is your turn, ask for a card using ASL correct topic/comment structure. For example,

$$\underline{\qquad\quad}^{t^*}\ \underline{\qquad\quad}^{q^*}$$
EIGHT, HAVE YOU

Be sure you sign your numbers and the non-manual grammatical markers correctly.

When asked for a card that you do not have, tell the player: (repeat the number),

$$\underline{\qquad}^{t}\qquad\qquad\underline{\qquad}^{t}$$
EIGHT, HAVE NOT... FISH, GO YOU

S/he will need to "fish" for the card by drawing a card from the pile. If s/he picks the card, s/he gets another turn.

If you have a card that a player requests, you **must** give it to him/her and then replace it with a card from the deck.

The first person to match all the cards in his/her hand wins.

*Note: The "t" indicates the topic of the sentence. Remember that your eyebrows are raised, head tilted slightly, and the sign is held a little longer. The "q" means you are asking a yes/no question. Remember to raise your eyebrows, tilt your head, and maintain direct eye contact while you wait for the answer.

LESSON EIGHT

8.12 Video Learning Experience

Bravo Family Visit

Viewing Goal: To improve your ASL comprehension skills by watching a Bravo family interaction.

Viewing Instructions: Watch the signed interaction and write a summary of the main points.

_____

_____

_____

_____

_____

_____

_____

_____

8.13 Comprehension Quiz

What Did You Understand?

Quiz Goal: To see how much of the Bravo family interaction you understood.

Quiz Instructions: Read and answer each question.

1. Anna's class has a(n) _____ lesson during our visit.
   - A. English
   - B. Math
   - C. Science
   - D. German

2. Did the student have the right answer to the first math problem?
   - A. Yes
   - B. No

LESSON EIGHT

3. One student uses a(n) _____ to get the right answer.

   A. Dictionary
   B. Encyclopedia
   C. Computer
   D. Calculator

4. Anna's class practices counting from one to thirty.

   A. True
   B. False

5. The sign for the number 17 is made up of what two signs?

   A. ONE and SEVEN
   B. TEN and SEVEN
   C. NINE and EIGHT
   D. TWO and FIFTEEN

8.14 Language Learning Instruction

Learning New Signs

Goal: To help you learn new ASL vocabulary.

Instructions: Your instructor will teach you new signs! Watch closely to learn what these signs mean and how they are produced.

In the space below, record any notes that will help you remember the signs.

_____

_____

_____

_____

_____

_____

_____

_____

_____

_____

_____

LESSON EIGHT

8.15 Video Learning Experience

LESSON ONE

Introduction to New Vocabulary

Viewing Goal: To help you learn new ASL vocabulary.

Viewing Instructions: Watch how Billy produces each sign. Be sure to notice the facial/body expressions. Copy the signs as Billy repeats each one.

Signs representing the following concepts are introduced:

directional verb

1. CLASS
2. ROOM
3. PAY-ATTENTION
4. PRINCIPAL
5. DREAM
6. SLEEP
7. BOY
8. GIRL
9. GOOD
10. BAD
11. NAME
12. MAYBE

8.16 Video Learning Experience

LESSON ONE

Bravo Family Visit

Viewing Goal: To improve your ASL comprehension skills by watching a Bravo family interaction.

Viewing Instructions: Watch the signed interaction and write a summary of the main points.

_____

_____

_____

_____

_____

_____

_____

_____

LESSON EIGHT

8.17 Comprehension Quiz

What Did You Understand?

Quiz Goal: To see how much of the Bravo family interaction you understood.

Quiz Instructions: Read and answer each question.

1. Who comes to visit Anna's classroom?
   Scott (principle)

2. What did Anna tell the visitor was wrong in her class?
   Not paying attention

3. When the visitor asks the students to take out a piece of paper, what do the students do?
   A. Take out paper
   B. Throw paper at the teacher
   C. Throw paper at each other
   D. They all started signing "No, no, no."

4. What does the visitor tell Anna about her students?
   _____

5. When she wakes up, what does Anna want her real teacher to do?
   _____
   _____

8.18 Video Learning Experience

Review Session

Viewing Goal: To help you remember how to produce the signs introduced in this lesson.

Viewing Instructions: Watch this video segment carefully to see how each sign is made, and take note of any hints given that might help you remember. You may want to copy the signs as you watch Billy.

After Billy reviews numbers 1-20, the following vocabulary is explained:

MATH   The old sign developed long ago meant TO-FIGURE. It has since become an initialized sign.

PLUS   This sign looks like the addition (plus) symbol.

MINUS   This sign looks like the subtraction (minus) symbol.

LESSON EIGHT

EQUAL	This sign shows it is not higher or lower, but the same (equal).
ADD	The one hand has something, the other hand adds to it.
COUNT	This is like counting coins in your hand. One, two, and so on.
CALCULATOR	This sign shows how a CALCULATOR is used.
TOGETHER	One hand is alone, the other is, too. Now we put them TOGETHER.
RIGHT	This sign is a symbol meaning RIGHT.
WRONG	This is also a symbol representing the concept of WRONG.
GOOD	You have already learned this sign on another tape. The palm orientation is up, meaning GOOD.
BAD	The palm orientation is the opposite of GOOD. It turns down as if you want to keep something away from you.
UNDERSTAND	This is like a light bulb that is connected to your head. When it goes on, you UNDERSTAND.
KNOW	You already have the information in your mind.
NAME	This sign is a symbol meaning NAME.
CLASS	This sign represents several people in a group.
ROOM	This sign shows the four walls of a room.
PAY-ATTENTION	This sign comes from the blinders which are placed on horses. It prevents them from looking from side to side, therefore it forces them to PAY-ATTENTION.
COME	This is an action sign showing where to go.
PRINCIPAL	One hand can represent a school, business or institution. The boss on top of it all is the PRINCIPAL.
DREAM	This sign is like the little white cloud you see in cartoons representing a dream.
SLEEP	This sign shows the eyes closing.
BOY	This sign represents the bill of a boy's baseball cap.
GIRL	Long ago, when the pioneers moved west, girls always wore bonnets. This sign comes from the strap tied under the chin.
MAYBE	One hand is YES, the other hand is NO. It's as if you are weighing the choices... MAYBE.

LESSON
EIGHT

8.19 Video Learning Experience

Cultural Notes

Viewing Goal: To learn about the cultural aspects of ASL.

Viewing Instructions: View the *Cultural Notes* segment carefully for the following:

I. The *Cultural Notes* segment discusses some of the benefits and disadvantages of attending a school for the Deaf.

   A. Benefits
   1. All the students are Deaf.
   2. Some teachers are Deaf, providing role models.
   3. Everyone knows and uses Sign Language.
   4. Establishes strong ties and connections to Deafculture.
   5. Promotes language development and growth.
   6. Provides a strong positive impact for Deaf children.
   7. Varied opportunities presented to all students equally:
      a. Sports
      b. Drama
      c. Field trips
      d. Social functions such as school dances
      e. Dormitories provide excellent opportunities for peer interaction
   8. Fosters Deaf leadership skills.
   9. Adult role models assist in development of self-esteem and language.

   B. A disadvantage of schools for the Deaf: families are often separated from the Deaf child because of distance.
   1. Some families move closer to schools for the Deaf.
   2. When children commute to school from home, they can still participate in social activities.

II. The first Deaf school in America was the American School for the Deaf. It is located in Hartford, Connecticut, and was established in 1817.

LESSON EIGHT

III. The Deaf community views schools for the Deaf with high regard:

A. Place of help.

B. Strong sense of belonging.

C. Warm memories.

D. Often considered "home."

IV. Deaf schools should not be viewed as a last educational option.

A. They are an equal option.

B. May be the best educational option for many children.

C. Schools for the Deaf should be respected and supported.

8.20 Experiential Activity

Special Guests

Activity Goal: To give you the opportunity to meet Deaf people and learn firsthand about their personal educational experiences.

Activity Instructions: Use the space below to record any information you find to be valuable or interesting. You may also want to record questions for the speaker(s) or your teacher.

_____

_____

_____

_____

_____

_____

_____

_____

_____

_____

LESSON EIGHT

Thought/Discussion Questions:

1. What did you learn from this panel?

   _____

   _____

   _____

2. How did each of the panel members feel about their educational experiences?

   _____

   _____

   _____

3. Did this panel change your opinion about any particular educational option(s)?

   _____

   _____

   _____

8.21 Video Learning Experience

LESSON ONE

Grammatical Notes

Viewing Goal: To learn about the grammatical aspects of ASL.

Viewing Instructions: Conceptual accuracy is the topic of this *Grammatical Notes* segment. View it carefully for the following:

A. Your choice and use of a sign must fit the conceptual meaning of what you are expressing. The signs you choose need to be selected based on their meaning, **not** based on English words. The following are examples of English words that represent several different meanings. Billy demonstrates how these multiple meanings are expressed by using conceptually accurate sign choices:

1. The word "like" has several meanings. Each meaning would be represented by a different sign:

   a. Like (related to feelings)

   b. Like (used to compare)

2. The word "play" has several meanings. Each meaning would be represented by a different sign:

   a. Play (violin)

   b. Play (drums)

   c. Play (piano)

   d. Play (tennis)

   e. Play (drama)

3. The word "right" has several meanings. Each meaning would be represented by a different sign:

   a. Right (I am right)

   b. Right (turn right)

   c. Right (my rights)

B. Conceptual accuracy is <u>not</u> based on English spelling or pronunciation.

Example: PAY-ATTENTION. The meaning is not related to paying money. The meaning is more closely related to focusing or concentrating, so the sign is produced as demonstrated on the video.

C. Conceptual accuracy is important! Correct conceptual meaning creates visual clarity and accuracy.

8.22 Experiential Activity

What Do You Mean?

Activity Goal: To choose ASL signs based on meaning.

Activity Instructions: English words may have several different meanings. ASL signs do not relate to English words, but to the meaning of what is being expressed.

Read each of the sentences below. Decide what sign you would use for the meaning of the word/concept that is printed in **bold**. A space has been provided for you to record your answers.

_____1. I have **gone** to the store before.

_____2. The food is all **gone**.

_____3. The light is **on** the table.

_____4. Turn **on** the light.

_____5. The book is **there**.

_____6. The book is **theirs**.

_____7. That **dog** is mine.

_____8. I am **dog** tired.

8.23 Video Learning Experience

LESSON ONE

Practice Session: Sentences

Viewing Goal: To improve your comprehension skills by watching sentences presented in ASL.

Viewing Instructions: Watch the signed sentences for comprehension. Remember to watch the face of each signer to see the facial/body expressions and the non-manual grammatical markers as well as the signs.

It is recommended that you copy each signed sentence when it is repeated.

In the space below, record any questions or notes you have regarding the sentences.

_____

_____

_____

_____

_____

_____

_____

8.24 Experiential Activity

Sign-A-Problem

Activity Goal: To practice understanding numbers and mathematical problems in ASL.

Activity Instructions: Use the spaces marked **My Problems** to create and write mathematical problems you will sign to your partner. The problems should be addition or subtraction, using the numbers 1-20. Solve each problem so you can check your partner's answers.

In the spaces marked **My Partner's Problems**, write the math problems that your partner signs to you. Complete the math. Sign your answers to one another. If there are errors, sign those problems again.

My Problems:

1. _____   6. _____
2. _____   7. _____
3. _____   8. _____
4. _____   9. _____
5. _____   10. _____

My Partner's Problems:

1. _____   6. _____
2. _____   7. _____
3. _____   8. _____
4. _____   9. _____
5. _____   10. _____

8.25 Video Learning Experience

LESSON ONE

Practice Session: Story

Viewing Goal: To improve your comprehension skills by watching a story presented in ASL.

Viewing Instructions: Watch the signed story for comprehension and write a summary to help you remember.

_____
_____
_____
_____
_____
_____
_____
_____
_____
_____
_____

LESSON EIGHT

8.26
Comprehension
Quiz

What Did You Understand?

Quiz Goal: To see how much of the signed story you understood.

Quiz Instructions: Read and answer each question below.

1. The character in the story was a _____.

   A. Hearing girl
   B. Hearing boy
   C. Deaf boy
   D. Deaf girl

2. The teacher was Deaf and signed fluently.

   A. True
   B. False

3. The student's family was Deaf.

   A. True
   B. False

4. The other children at school were _____.

   A. Deaf and hearing
   B. Hearing
   C. Older
   D. Deaf

5. According to the story, the student was also a
   _____.

   A. Cub scout
   B. Baseball player
   C. Teacher
   D. Swimmer

LESSON EIGHT

8.27 Homework Assignment

A Dramatic Day at School!

Homework Goal: To practice using the vocabulary learned in Lessons Seven and Eight and the grammatical principles taught in all previous lessons.

Homework Instructions: Work with your group to prepare a short skit that shows a *Dramatic Day At School!*

Use as many of the signs you learned in Lessons Seven and Eight as possible. Be sure to include: yes/no-questions; wh-questions; adjective placement; negation; topic/comment structure; parameters of sign production; directional verbs; and conceptual sign choices.

Your instructor will let you know when this drama will be performed in class. All members of the group must have signing roles in the drama.

This is your chance to be *creative* and *dramatic*!

8.28 Post-test

What Do You Know Now?

Post-test Goal: To assess your mastery of the lesson objectives.

Post-test Introduction: This test has three sections:

Section One: The Comprehension section tests your ability to understand ASL.

Section Two: The Culture and Grammar section tests your knowledge of the material presented in the *Cultural* and *Grammatical Notes.*

Section Three: The Expressive portion tests your ability to use ASL.

Simply follow the instructions for each section.

Good luck!

Lesson 9
DOLLAR SIGNS

9.2 Homework Review

A Dramatic Day at School!

Activity Goal: To show the results of your homework assignment.

Activity Instructions: Your group will perform its skit, *A Dramatic Day at School!*, as assigned in Lesson Eight. Remember to include the school-related vocabulary introduced in Lessons Seven and Eight as well as the grammatical features you learned in Lessons One through Eight.

While other groups perform their skits, pay close attention and practice your ASL comprehension skills! Use ASL to ask questions about your classmates' *Dramatic Days at School!*

9.3 Pretest

What Do You Know?

Pretest Goal: To see how much you already know about what will be taught in this lesson.

Pretest Instructions: Read and answer each question.

1. In the past, employment options for Deaf people have been limited to jobs involving menial labor.

   (A) True
   B. False

2. The telephone has been and still is a complete communication barrier in the workplace for Deaf people.

   A. True
   (B.) False

3. What type of jobs are available to Deaf people today?
   ~~menial labor~~ Anything

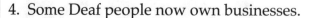

4. Some Deaf people now own businesses.

   (A.) True
   B. False

5. The sign for ONE DOLLAR is made with a different movement than the sign for the number ONE.

   (A.) True
   B. False

6. Signs for dollar amounts of $10 or more are made differently than the signs for $9 or less.

   (A.) True
   B. False

7. The sign for "bank" is actually a fingerspelled loan sign.

   (A.) True
   B. False

9.4 Lesson Objectives

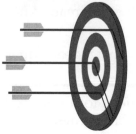

Planning for Success

Goal: To see what you will learn by the end of this lesson.

Instructions: Read the objectives below.

Upon completing this VideoCourse lesson, you will be able to...

1. Recognize and accurately produce the ASL vocabulary introduced in this and all previous lessons.

2. Compare the employment opportunities available to Deaf workers in the past with those opportunities available today.

3. Explain why the telephone is less of a barrier for Deaf workers today than it was in the past, particularly in regards to employment or owning a business.

4. Recognize and accurately produce number signs related to money.

LESSON NINE

9.5 Lesson Focus

The Silent Games

Activity Goal: To experience playing games with money using ASL.

Activity Instructions: Your group will play a game involving money. During the game, communicate using ASL, gestures, mime, and fingerspelling - but do not use your voice!

Follow the game rules supplied with each game. Have fun and good luck!

Thought/Discussion Questions

1. What are some signs related to money that would have been useful to know during this activity?

   _____

   _____

   _____

2. How did it feel to be limited in your ability to communicate?

   _____

   _____

   _____

3. What are some techniques Deaf people could use to communicate about money with people who don't sign?

   _____

   _____

   _____

LESSON NINE

9.6 Video Learning Experience

Bravo Family Visit

Viewing Goal: To improve your ASL comprehension by watching a Bravo family interaction.

Viewing Instructions: Watch the interaction with Scott and Dad at the bank. Billy helps you understand what this lesson is about.

In the space below, write a summary of the main points to help you remember the interaction.

_____

_____

_____

_____

_____

_____

_____

9.7 Language Learning Instruction

Learning New Signs

Goal: To help you learn new ASL vocabulary.

Instructions: Your instructor will teach you new signs! Watch closely to learn what these signs mean and how they are produced.

In the space below, record any notes to help you remember the signs.

_____

_____

_____

_____

_____

_____

_____

_____

_____

9.8 Video Learning Experience

Introduction to New Vocabulary

Viewing Goal: To help you learn new ASL vocabulary.

Viewing Instructions: Watch how Billy produces each sign. Be sure to notice the facial/body expressions. Copy the signs as Billy repeats each one.

Signs representing the following concepts are introduced in this video segment:

1. BANK
2. MONEY
3. SAVE
4. SAVINGS
5. INTEREST

6. DEPOSIT
7. SLOW
8. HOW-MUCH
9. THOUSAND
10. THREE+THOUSAND

9.9 Video Learning Experience

Bravo Family Visit

Viewing Goal: To improve your ASL comprehension by watching a Bravo family interaction.

Viewing Instructions: Watch the signed interaction and write a summary of the main points.

_____

_____

_____

_____

_____

_____

_____

_____

LESSON NINE

9.10 Comprehension Quiz

What Did You Understand?

Quiz Goal: To see how much of the Bravo family interaction you understood.

Quiz Instructions: Read and answer each question.

1. What does Dad want to do at the bank?
   - A. He wants open a savings account.
   - B. He wants to make a deposit to his checking account.
   - C. He wants to apply for a job as a bank teller.
   - D. He wants to open a checking account.

2. How much money is Dad depositing?
   $3,000⁰⁰

3. What does Scott want to do instead of wait for Dad at the bank?
   Eat ice cream

4. Why is Scott sent to sit someplace else?
   being rude ?

5. What does Scott wish?
   Wish I could sign

9.11 Video Learning Experience

LESSON NINE

Communication Strategies

Viewing Goal: To help you learn communication strategies for interactions between signing and non-signing people.

Viewing Instructions: Watch the video carefully to learn important communication strategies.

Billy mentions four communication strategies used by the bank teller when she was communicating with Dad:

1. Maintain direct and consistent eye contact.

2. Learn new signs as you are communicating.

3. Write things down to be sure communication is clear and to avoid misunderstandings.

4. Be patient, friendly, and respectful of the communication needs of other people.

LESSON NINE

9.12 Experiential Activity

Crossing the Communication Barrier

Activity Goal: To help you apply the communication strategies taught in this lesson.

Activity Instructions: In small groups, role-play a banking situation. One person in the group acts as the bank teller while another role-plays a Deaf customer.

Remaining group members will observe and evaluate the role-players' communication strategies.

The bank teller:

1. Maintained direct and consistent eye contact.
   Yes _✓_ No ___

2. Learned new signs as s/he communicated.
   Yes _✓_ No ___

3. Wrote things down to be sure communication was clear.
   Yes _✓_ No ___

4. Was patient and friendly and respectful of the communication needs of the customer.
   Yes _✓_ No ___

9.13 Language Learning Instruction

Learning New Signs

Goal: To help you learn new ASL vocabulary.

Instructions: Your instructor will teach you new signs! Watch closely to learn what these signs mean and how they are produced.

In the space below, record any notes to help you remember the signs.

_____

_____

_____

_____

_____

_____

_____

_____

_____

LESSON NINE

9.14 Video Learning Experience

LESSON NINE

Introduction to New Vocabulary

Viewing Goal: To help you learn new ASL vocabulary.

Viewing Instructions: Watch how Billy produces each sign. Be sure to notice the facial/body expressions. Copy the signs as Billy repeats each one.

Signs representing the following concepts are introduced:

1. ONE+HUNDRED
2. WITHDRAW
3. BALANCE
4. CHARGE/FEE
5. MORE *value* *account*
6. ALL
7. PEOPLE
8. FAST
9. SAME *me too*
10. PERCENT

9.15 Video Learning Experience

LESSON NINE

Bravo Family Visit

Viewing Goal: To improve your ASL comprehension by watching a Bravo family interaction.

Viewing Instructions: Watch the signed interaction and write a summary of the main points.

_____
_____
_____
_____
_____
_____
_____
_____

9.16
Comprehension Quiz

What Did You Understand?

Quiz Goal: To see how much of the Bravo family interaction you understood.

Quiz Instructions: Read and answer each question below.

1. The teller explained the difference between which two types of accounts?

   A. Checking and savings
   B. Money market and checking
   C. Money market and regular savings
   D. Checking and CD

2. Which type of account does Dad decide to open?

   A. Money market
   B. Checking
   C. Regular savings
   D. CD

3. What is different between the real teller and the teller in Scott's dream?

   A. Scott's teller is nicer.
   B. Scott's teller is Deaf.
   C. Scott's teller is hearing.
   D. Scott's teller gives him ice cream.

4. In Scott's dream, the banking transaction was much slower because Dad and the teller used ASL.

   A. True
   B. False

LESSON NINE

9.17 Language Learning Instruction

Learning New Signs

Goal: To help you learn new ASL vocabulary.

Instructions: Your instructor will teach you new signs! Watch closely to learn what these signs mean and how they are produced.

In the space below, record any notes to help you remember the signs.

_____

_____

_____

_____

_____

_____

_____

_____

_____

_____

9.18 Video Learning Experience

Introduction to New Vocabulary

Viewing Goal: To help you learn new ASL vocabulary.

Viewing Instructions: Watch how Billy produces each sign. Be sure to notice the facial/body expressions. Copy the signs as Billy repeats each one.

Signs representing the following concepts are introduced:

1. ADDRESS
2. NUMBER
3. TELEPHONE
4. SOCIAL-SECURITY
5. BIRTHDAY
6. DRIVE
7. LICENSE
8. SIGNATURE
9. CHECK
10. DOLLAR
11. ONE-DOLLAR
12. FIVE-DOLLAR
13. TEN+DOLLAR
14. TWENTY+DOLLAR
15. FIFTY+DOLLAR
16. MILLION

9.19 Experiential Activity

Tic-Tac-Dough

Activity Goal: To help you recognize the new ASL vocabulary.

Activity Instructions: Your instructor will divide the class into two teams (Team X and Team O).

You will see a Tic-Tac-Dough (similar to Tic-Tac-Toe) grid on the board. Two players from Team X will go to the board. The first player will choose a picture and show the correct sign to the second player. The second player must point to the right picture and repeat the sign. If both players have produced the sign correctly, they can place an X on the correct square.

The two teams will take turns until one team gets three marks in a row.

Good luck and have fun!

9.20 Video Learning Experience

Bravo Family Visit

Viewing Goal: To improve your ASL comprehension by watching a Bravo family interaction.

Viewing Instructions: Watch the signed interaction for comprehension and write a summary of the main points.

_____

_____

_____

_____

_____

_____

_____

_____

LESSON NINE

9.21 Comprehension Quiz

What Did You Understand?

Quiz Goal: To see how much of the Bravo family interaction you understood.

Quiz Instructions: Read and answer each question below.

1. The bank teller asks Dad for his address, telephone number, and the amount of his deposit.

   Ⓐ True
   B. False

2. The bank teller tells Scott he needs to sign the form.

   A. True
   B. False

3. Instead of going for ice cream, Scott tells his Dad that he wants to _____.

   A. Go home
   B. Go to the park
   Ⓒ Make a deposit
   D. Make a withdrawal

4. When Dad wakes Scott up, he tells him it's time _____.

   A. To wake up
   B. To go home
   C. To go to another bank
   Ⓓ To go get ice cream

5. As Scott and Dad leave the bank, the Deaf bank teller tells Scott to _____.

   Ⓐ Enjoy his ice cream
   B. Have a nice day
   C. Be careful
   D. Save his money

LESSON NINE

9.22 Video Learning Experience

Cultural Notes

Viewing Goal: To learn about the cultural aspects of ASL.

Viewing Instructions: View the *Cultural Notes* segment carefully for the following:

I. Employment options for Deaf people:

   A. Historically, Deaf people were limited to areas such as assembly, printing, post office jobs, sewing, other menial labor work.

   B. Today, options have increased. Deaf people hold positions as: artists; directors; dancers; photographers; counselors; secretaries; teachers; lawyers; doctors; etc.

   C. Access to the workplace has improved. Some Deaf people actually own their own businesses.

II. The telephone is less of a barrier because of:

   A. Relay services

   B. Professional interpreters

   C. Technology such as TTYs, email, videophones, etc.

9.23 Video Learning Experience

Grammatical Notes

Viewing Goal: To learn about the grammatical aspects of ASL.

Viewing Instructions: View the *Grammatical Notes* segment carefully for the following:

When the signs representing numbers are related to money, the movement of the sign changes.

   A. The signs for the numbers 1 - 9, when showing dollar amounts, move in a twisting motion from the wrist. This movement lets you know it is a dollar amount.

   B. Billy demonstrates the production of the signs, $1- $9 in this video segment.

   C. Dollar amounts for $10 and higher are signed the same way as regular number signs, but are followed by the sign for DOLLAR.

9.24
Experiential
Activity

Is the Price Right?

Activity Goal: To improve your ASL comprehension skills.

Activity Instructions: You will see a signer describing the items below and their correct prices in ASL. Find the picture of each item and write the correct price on its price tag.

LESSON
NINE

9.25 Experiential Activity

Dollar-to-Dollar

Activity Goal: To help you recognize and produce dollar amounts.

Activity Instructions: You have just learned how to sign dollar amounts. In the spaces below, marked **My Dollars**, select ten of the dollar amounts listed below. Take turns signing the dollar amounts with a partner. Record the various amounts your partner signs to you in the column marked **My Partner's Dollars**. Check each other when you are finished to see how well you understood the signs.

Dollar amounts: $1.00 - $9.00

$10.00 - $20.00

$50.00

$100.00

$1,000

$3,000

$1,000,000 (ONE+MILLION)

My Dollars	**My Partner's Dollars**
1._____	1._____
2._____	2._____
3._____	3._____
4._____	4._____
5._____	5._____
6._____	6._____
7._____	7._____
8._____	8._____
9._____	9._____
10._____	10._____

LESSON NINE

9.26 Video Learning Experience

LESSON NINE

Review Session

Viewing Goal: To help you remember how to produce the signs introduced in this lesson.

Viewing Instructions: Watch this video segment carefully to see how each sign is made. Take note of hints that will help you remember. You may want to copy the signs as you watch Billy.

The following are the vocabulary and explanations offered in this video segment:

B-A-N-K	This is a fingerspelled loan sign. This means that the fingerspelled sign is borrowed from the fingerspelled word. Due to the production and fast movement, it is actually considered a sign.
SAVINGS	Money is put into a place where it adds up and is not spent.
MONEY	This sign is like taking the money and placing it in your hand.
HOW-MUCH	This sign is like throwing money into the air and counting it to see HOW-MUCH.
DEPOSIT	You take the money to the bank and you put it in the account.
FIFTY	This is a compound sign using the signs FIVE+ZERO.
ONE+HUNDRED	The "C" handshape represents the Roman numeral symbol for 100.
ONE+THOUSAND	This sign follows the Roman numeral "M" for 1,000.
THREE+THOUSAND	This is a compound sign using the signs THREE+THOUSAND.
MILLION	This sign also follows the Roman numeral. It represents a thousand thousands.
INTEREST	One hand represents a savings account. As you earn money, it is added to the top of your account. The other hand represents the INTEREST.
MONEY+MARKET	The "M"+"M" represents the two words "money" and "market." It is abbreviated so it is not necessary to fingerspell it.
SLOW	This sign shows how a glacier moves - very slowly.
MORE	One hand represents what you have. The other hand is giving you more of it.
ALL	There are things in front of you and you take all of them.

PEOPLE	When there are many persons, it is shown with this sign for PEOPLE.
FAST	This sign shows how a bullet leaves a gun. It's very FAST.
WITHDRAW	One hand represents money in an account. The other hand shows you're removing it or taking it out.
BALANCE	Two signs are described. 1. BALANCE: meaning is there a positive or negative balance. 2. BALANCE: this represents the "money left in the bank.
PERCENT	This sign follows the way we actually write the symbol for percent (%).
SAME/ME-TOO	The movement of this sign between us means you and I are the SAME.
LIMIT	This sign shows the upper and lower limits.
ADDRESS	This comes from the sign TO-LIVE which is a verb. When we do the movement twice, it becomes the noun, ADDRESS.
NUMBER	This sign comes from the old symbol for number (#). Over time, the handshape and movement have evolved to the current sign.
TELEPHONE	This sign follows the shape and the use of a telephone.
SOCIAL+SECURITY	In order to avoid fingerspelling those long words over and over, we abbreviate them "S" + "S."
BIRTHDAY	This sign represents a child being born.
DRIVE	How do you drive a car? You use a steering wheel.
LICENSE	This sign follows the shape of a license.
SIGNATURE	You put your name down on a piece of paper. This sign represents that action.
CHECK	This sign follows the shape of a check.
DOLLAR	This sign follows the shape of an actual dollar.
SET-UP	You can SET-UP or OPEN an account. Either sign is fine.
REGULAR	If something happens on a regular basis, it occurs again and again, it is REGULAR.
FILL-OUT-FORM	One hand represents the piece of paper with all the lines on it. The other hand is filling in all those lines.
LEAVE	This sign shows that something is there that you don't touch or take...you LEAVE it.
MONTH	This sign comes from the grid of a calendar and represents four weeks.
MONTHLY	You have one month on a calendar. When you turn the page to the next month and the next...it is MONTHLY.

LESSON NINE

9.27 Video Learning Experience

Practice Session: Sentences

Viewing Goal: To improve your ASL comprehension skills by watching signed sentences.

Viewing Instructions: Watch the signed sentences for comprehension. Remember to watch the face of each signer to see the facial/body expressions and the non-manual grammatical markers as well as the signs.

It is recommended that you copy each signed sentence when it is repeated.

In the space below, record any questions or notes you have regarding the sentences.

_____

_____

_____

_____

_____

_____

9.28 Video Learning Experience

Practice Session: Story

Viewing Goal: To improve your ASL comprehension by watching a story presented in ASL.

Viewing Instructions: Watch the signed story for comprehension. In the space below, write a summary to help you remember the story.

_____

_____

_____

_____

_____

_____

_____

9.29
Comprehension Quiz

What Did You Understand?

Quiz Goal: To see how much of the signed story you understood.

Quiz Instructions: Read and answer each question below.

1. What was the special event that happened in the story?
   _____
   _____

2. What did the signer get for the special event?
   _____
   _____

3. Who gave him the gift?
   _____
   _____

4. Where did he take his gift first? Why?
   _____
   _____

5. What did the signer finally do with his gift?
   _____
   _____

9.30
Experiential Activity

The Silent Games: Revisited

Activity Goal: To use your new ASL vocabulary for playing the *Silent Games*.

Activity Instructions: Your group will play a game that involves play money again. During the game, use ASL (no voices needed!).

Try to use as many of your new ASL vocabulary words as you can. You can also use gestures, fingerspelling, mime, pointing, etc.

See if your communication skills have improved!

Have fun!!

LESSON NINE

9.31 Homework Assignment

Silent Auction

Homework Goal: To participate in an auction conducted in ASL.

Homework Instructions: Your class will have a *Silent Auction* where you can buy and sell items using play money.

Remember to bring some individually-wrapped items that your classmates might be interested in buying, such as snack cakes; candy; canned soda; juice boxes; pencils; chips; crackers; notebooks; or magazines.

Be prepared to use ASL to present an exciting sales pitch describing the items you have for sale.

Your classmates will bid on each item. The highest bidder will pay with play money from the board games in previous activities.

Note: You will all begin with the same amount of play money. See who can buy the most items with the money.

9.32 Post-test Introduction

What Do You Know Now?

Post-test Goal: To assess your mastery of the lesson objectives.

Post-test Introduction: This test has three sections.

Section One: The Comprehension section tests your ability to understand ASL.

Section Two: The Culture and Grammar section tests your knowledge of the material presented in the *Cultural* and *Grammatical Notes*.

Section Three: The Expressive portion tests your ability to use ASL.

Simply follow the instructions for each section.

Good luck!

LESSON NINE

Lesson 10
REVIEW & PRACTICE SESSION

10.2 Homework Review

Silent Auction

Activity Goal: To show the results of your homework assignment.

Activity Instructions: It's time for the Silent Auction! Take turns signing the "sales pitch" you prepared for each of your auction items. Your instructor will serve as the auctioneer.

You will be given play money. Bid (in ASL) on the items you want… the items will go to the highest bidder! See who can buy the most with the play money.

Good luck, and remember this is a *Silent* Auction!

10.3 Lesson Objectives

Planning for Success

Goal: To see what you will learn by the end of this lesson.

Instructions: Read the objectives below.

Upon completing this VideoCourse lesson, you will be able to...

1. Recognize and accurately produce the ASL vocabulary introduced in Lessons Six, Seven, Eight, and Nine.

2. Demonstrate knowledge of the cultural information presented in Lessons Six, Seven, Eight, and Nine.

3. Recognize and apply the grammatical features presented in Lessons Six, Seven, Eight, and Nine.

4. Accurately use the ASL vocabulary and grammatical features presented in Lessons Six, Seven, Eight, and Nine in sentences, dialogues, and stories.

LESSON TEN

10.4 Video Learning Experience

Lesson Introduction

Viewing Goal: To help you prepare for this review session.

Viewing Instructions: Billy will explain what to expect from this *Review & Practice Session*.

Pay attention to what Billy is signing, but also notice *how* he expresses these ideas with facial/body expression, non-manual grammatical markers, and use of space. Perhaps you will learn a few more signs!

In the space below, write any notes or questions you may have.

_____

_____

_____

_____

_____

_____

_____

_____

10.5 Experiential Activity

Color Commands

Activity Goal: To help you remember the ASL vocabulary learned in Lesson Six.

Activity Instructions: Work with a partner and decide which of the two pictures below you will each use. Select an object or person from your partner's picture and use ASL to instruct your partner how to color the items in the picture s/he selected. When this is completed, switch roles.

You can choose from the following colors:

BLACK	ORANGE	RED	GOLD
WHITE	TEN	YELLOW	PINK
SILVER	BLUE	TAN	BROWN

Note: If you don't have the right color marker or crayon, write the name of the color on each item in the picture.

Partner A's Picture:

Partner B's Picture:

10.6 Video Learning Experience

LESSON TEN

Lesson Six Review: Vocabulary

Viewing Goal: To help you review the ASL vocabulary from Lesson Six.

Viewing Instructions: Watch the Lesson Six vocabulary review while you copy the signs. Raise your hand if there is a sign you do not remember, and your instructor will help you.

Signs representing the following concepts are reviewed in this video segment:

1. ORANGE
2. BLUE
3. GREEN
4. RED
5. YELLOW
6. PURPLE
7. WHITE
8. BROWN
9. SILVER
10. GOLD
11. PINK
12. BLACK
13. TAN

Note: A review of fingerspelling is also provided in this video segment. Billy fingerspells each letter of the alphabet. It is suggested that you copy Billy as he produces each letter.

LESSON TEN

10.7 Video Learning Experience

Lesson Six Review: Sentences

Viewing Goal: To improve your comprehension skills by watching sentences presented in ASL.

Viewing Instructions: Watch the signed sentences for comprehension. Remember to watch the face of each signer to see the facial/body expressions and the non-manual grammatical markers as well as the signs.

It is recommended that you copy each signed sentence when it is repeated.

In the space below, record any questions or notes you have regarding the sentences.

_____

_____

_____

_____

_____

10.8 Video Learning Experience

Lesson Six Review: Fingerspelling Practice

Viewing Goal: To improve your fingerspelling comprehension skills.

Viewing Instructions: Watch the fingerspelled words for comprehension. Remember to watch the face of each signer to see the facial/body expressions and the non-manual grammatical markers as well as the fingerspelled words.

Sound out the letters the way you would if you were reading. Notice the patterns of letter combinations such as IN, AT, AP, OT and OY.

In the space below, record notes or questions you may have.

_____

_____

_____

_____

_____

10.9 Experiential Activity

Flying Fingers

Activity Goal: To help improve your fingerspelling skills.

Activity Instructions: With a partner, take turns fingerspelling words from the list below. When it is your partner's turn to fingerspell, watch carefully and fingerspell the words back to him/her.

C-A-T	T-E-D	S-I-T	N-A-P	M-I-K-E	B-O-B	N-A-N-C-Y
B-A-T	N-E-D	B-I-T	C-A-P	L-I-K-E	C-O-B	F-A-N-C-Y
S-A-T	F-E-D	K-I-T	Z-A-P	P-I-K-E	C-O-N	C-L-A-N-C-Y
M-A-T	B-E-D	Z-I-T	L-A-P	T-I-K-E	D-O-N	D-A-N-C-Y

When you have practiced the above letter combinations, practice with names of places and people you know while your partner fingerspells them back to you.

10.10 Video Learning Experience

Lesson Six Review: Practice Dialogue

Viewing Goal: To improve your comprehension skills by watching a dialogue presented in ASL.

Viewing Instructions: Watch the signed dialogue for comprehension. With a partner, create a similar dialogue about the colors of your own home.

_____

_____

_____

_____

_____

_____

_____

_____

_____

_____

LESSON TEN

10.11 Video Learning Experience

Bravo Family Revisited

Viewing Goal: To reinforce your ASL comprehension skills by reviewing a Bravo family interaction from Lesson Six.

Viewing Instructions: Watch the signed interaction for review and take notes or write a summary.

_____

_____

_____

_____

10.12 Experiential Activity

Crossword Puzzle

Activity Goal: To help you remember the ASL vocabulary learned in Lesson Seven.

Activity Instructions: In your group, select one person to be the "puzzle leader." That person will sign all the clues to the puzzle below. Watch carefully, and select the word which best matches each sign's meaning and fits in the correct boxes in the puzzle. See if your group can be the first to correctly complete the puzzle and earn the title of "Puzzle Masters."

10.13 Video Learning Experience

Lesson Seven Review: Vocabulary

Viewing Goal: To help you review the ASL vocabulary from Lesson Seven.

Viewing Instructions: Watch the Lesson Seven vocabulary review while you copy the signs. Raise your hand if there is a sign you do not recognize, and your instructor will help you.

Signs representing the following concepts are reviewed in this video segment:

1. SCHOOL	11. THERE	21. WHO
2. TEACHER	12. GROW-UP	22. PENCIL
3. BOOK	13. TEACH	23. PAPER
4. READ	14. LEARN	24. GOOD
5. SIT	15. STUDENT	25. NEED
6. TIRED	16. STUDY	26. PLEASE
7. SORRY	17. GIVE	27 HAVE
8. FLOWER	18. PLAY	28. WANT
9. PICK+FLOWER	19. WHAT-WRONG	29. LATE
10. HERE	20. NOT	30. FINISH

10.14 Video Learning Experience

Lesson Seven Review: Sentences

Viewing Goal: To improve your comprehension skills by watching sentences presented in ASL.

Viewing Instructions: Watch the signed sentences for comprehension. Remember to watch the face of each signer to see the facial/body expressions and the non-manual grammatical markers as well as the signs.

It is recommended that you copy each signed sentence when it is repeated.

In the space below, record any questions or notes you have regarding the sentences.

_____

_____

_____

_____

_____

LESSON TEN

10.15 Video Learning Experience

Lesson Seven Review: Practice Dialogue

Viewing Goal: To improve your comprehension skills by watching a dialogue presented in ASL.

Viewing Instructions: Watch the signed dialogue for comprehension and write a summary in the space provided.

_____

_____

_____

_____

_____

_____

_____

_____

10.16 Experiential Activity

Dynamic-Duo Dialogue

Activity Goal: To improve your expressive and receptive ASL skills.

Activity Instructions: Work with a partner to create a dialogue using the Lesson Seven vocabulary (see the Sign Illustration Section for Lesson Seven vocabulary). Use ASL (no voices needed!) and be sure each person takes at least five turns.

Be prepared to share your dialogue with the class!

In the space below, record ideas or notes regarding the dialogue.

_____

_____

_____

_____

_____

_____

_____

_____

10.17 Video Learning Experience

LESSON TEN

Bravo Family Revisited

Viewing Goal: To reinforce your ASL expressive and receptive skills by reviewing a Bravo family interaction from Lesson Seven.

Viewing Instructions: Watch the Bravo family interaction. Be prepared to work with your classmates to recreate the "fight" over the book. Be sure to use directional verbs as shown in the video.

10.18 Experiential Activity

Matchmaker

Activity Goal: To help you remember some of the ASL vocabulary learned in Lesson Eight.

Activity Instructions: Look at the illustrations below. Draw a line from the sign illustration to the picture that best matches its meaning.

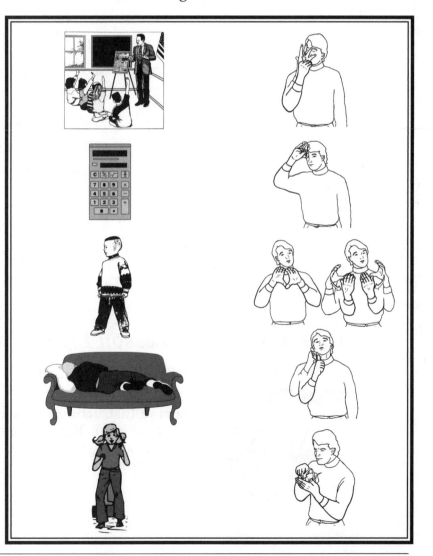

LESSON TEN

10.19 Video Learning Experience

Lesson Eight Review: Vocabulary

Viewing Goal: To help you review the ASL vocabulary from Lesson Eight.

Viewing Instructions: Watch the Lesson Eight vocabulary review while you copy the signs. Raise your hand if there is a sign you do not recognize, and your instructor will help you.

Signs representing the following concepts are reviewed in this video segment:

1. #1	16. #16	31. ADD
2. #2	17. #17	32. TOGETHER
3. #3	18. #18	33. UNDERSTAND
4. #4	19. #19	34. CLASS
5. #5	20. #20	35. ROOM
6. #6	21. MATH	36. PAY-ATTENTION
7. #7	22. PLUS	37. PRINCIPAL
8. #8	23. MINUS/NEGATIVE	38. DREAM
9. #9	24. EQUAL/FAIR	39. SLEEP
10. #10	25. RIGHT/CORRECT	40. BOY
11. #11	26. WRONG/INCORRECT	41. GIRL
12. #12	27. KNOW	42. GOOD
13. #13	28. CALCULATOR	43. BAD
14. #14	29. COUNT	44. NAME
15. #15	30. COME	45. MAYBE

10.20 Video Learning Experience

Lesson Eight Review: Sentences

Viewing Goal: To improve your comprehension skills by watching sentences presented in ASL.

Viewing Instructions: Watch the signed sentences for comprehension. Remember to watch the face of each signer to see the facial/body expressions and the non-manual grammatical markers as well as the signs.

It is recommended that you copy each signed sentence when it is repeated.

In the space below, record any questions or notes you have regarding the sentences.

_____

_____

_____

_____

_____

_____

_____

_____

_____

10.21 Video Learning Experience

Lesson Eight Review: Practice Dialogue

Viewing Goal: To improve your comprehension skills by watching a dialogue presented in ASL.

Viewing Instructions: Watch the signed dialogue for comprehension and write a summary in the space provided.

_____

_____

_____

_____

_____

_____

_____

_____

_____

LESSON TEN

10.22 Experiential Activity

Dynamic-Duo Dialogue

Activity Goal: To improve your expressive and receptive ASL skills.

Activity Instructions: Work with a partner to create a dialogue using the Lesson Eight vocabulary (see activity 10.19 for the vocabulary list). Use ASL (no voices needed!) and be sure each person takes at least four turns.

Be prepared to share your dialogue with the class!

In the space below, record any ideas or notes regarding the dialogue.

_____

_____

_____

_____

_____

_____

_____

_____

10.23 Video Learning Experience

Bravo Family Revisited

Viewing Goal: To reinforce your ASL comprehension skills by reviewing a Bravo family interaction from Lesson Eight.

Viewing Instructions: Watch the *Bravo Family Revisited* for review. Be prepared to use ASL to summarize what happened in this video segment!

_____

_____

_____

_____

_____

_____

_____

_____

LESSON TEN

10.24 Experiential Activity

Point and Sign

Activity Goal: To improve your skills with the ASL vocabulary introduced in Lesson Nine.

Activity Instructions: Using the pictures below, follow your teacher's instructions to practice your signing skills.

LESSON TEN

10.25 Video Learning Experience

Lesson Nine Review: Vocabulary

Viewing Goal: To help you review the ASL vocabulary from Lesson Nine.

Viewing Instructions: Watch the Lesson Nine vocabulary review. Raise your hand if there is a sign you do not recognize, and your instructor will help you.

Signs representing the following concepts are reviewed in this video segment:

1. BANK	13. BALANCE	25. BIRTHDAY
2. MONEY	14. CHARGE/FEE	26. DRIVE
3. SAVE	15. MORE	27. LICENSE
4. SAVINGS	16. ALL	28. SIGNATURE
5. INTEREST	17. PEOPLE	29. CHECK
6. DEPOSIT	18. FAST	30. DOLLAR
7. SLOW	19. SAME	31. $1.00
8. HOW-MUCH	20. PERCENT	32. $5.00
9. THOUSAND	21. ADDRESS	33. $10.00
10. THREE+THOUSAND	22. NUMBER	34. $20.00
11. 100	23. TELEPHONE	35. $50.00
12. WITHDRAW	24. SOCIAL-SECURITY	36. MILLION

10.26 Video Learning Experience

Lesson Nine Review: Sentences

Viewing Goal: To improve your comprehension skills by watching sentences presented in ASL.

Viewing Instructions: Watch the signed sentences for comprehension. Remember to watch the face of each signer to see the facial/body expressions and the non-manual grammatical markers as well as the signs.

It is recommended that you copy each signed sentence when it is repeated.

In the space below, record any questions or notes you have regarding the sentences.

_____

_____

_____

_____

LESSON TEN

10.27 Video Learning Experience

Lesson Nine Review: Practice Dialogue

Viewing Goal: To improve your comprehension skills by watching a dialogue presented in ASL.

Viewing Instructions: Watch the signed dialogue for comprehension and write a summary in the space provided.

_____

_____

_____

_____

_____

_____

_____

_____

10.28 Experiential Activity

Dynamic-Duo Dialogue

Activity Goal: To improve your expressive and receptive ASL skills.

Activity Instructions: Work with a partner to create a dialogue using the vocabulary from Lesson Nine (see the Sign Illustration Section for Lesson Nine vocabulary). Use ASL (no voices needed!) and be sure each person takes at least four turns.

Be prepared to share your dialogue with the class!

In the space below, record any ideas or notes you have regarding the dialogue.

_____

_____

_____

_____

_____

_____

_____

_____

10.29 Video Learning Experience

Bravo Family Revisited

Viewing Goal: To reinforce your ASL comprehension skills by reviewing a Bravo family interaction from Lesson Nine.

Viewing Instructions: Watch the *Bravo Family Revisited* for review and write a summary of the main points.

_____

_____

_____

_____

_____

_____

10.30 Experiential Activity

Pictures in the Air

Activity Goal: To improve your expressive and comprehension skills.

Activity Instructions: Your instructor will divide the class into four groups and assign each group one of the pictures below.

Based on your picture, work with your group to create a skit using ASL (no voice!). Your group will have time to prepare and practice your skit and then show it to the whole class.

10.31 Video Learning Experience

Lessons Six Thru Nine Review: Cultural Notes

Viewing Goal: To help you review the cultural aspects of ASL presented in Lessons Six, Seven, Eight, and Nine.

Viewing Instructions: Answer the questions below to see how well you remember these cultural aspects of ASL. When you are finished, watch the video. Billy will provide you with the answers to correct your work.

1. Why is it so important to sign when a Deaf adult or child is around?

   _____

   _____

   _____

2. When parents are considering educational options for their Deaf child, what two issues must be considered?

   _____

   _____

3. List four reasons why going to a school for the Deaf is beneficial to a Deaf child.

   _____

   _____

   _____

   _____

4. Can you think of three ways the telephone is accessible to a Deaf person?

   _____

   _____

   _____

5. When a Deaf person is considering employment possibilities, is there one specific job suited for Deaf workers?

   _____

   _____

   _____

LESSON TEN

10.32 Video Learning Experience

LESSON TEN

Lessons Six Thru Nine Review: Grammatical Notes

Viewing Goal: To help you apply the grammatical aspects of ASL presented in Lessons Six through Nine.

Viewing Instructions: Answer the questions below to see how well you remember these grammatical aspects of ASL. When you are finished, watch the video. Billy will provide the answers so you can see how well you did.

1. In American Sign Language, each sign has four main components or parameters. One is a distinct handshape. Can you name the other three?

    1) Distinct handshape

    2) _____

    3) _____

    4) _____

2. In the video, Dad uses the sign GIVE. What information was added to the verb GIVE by the use of directionality?

    _____

    _____

3. You saw several examples of sign choices based on meaning (right/correct vs. right/direction). What do we call this principle?

    _____

4. Practice signing the amounts $1-$9 with Billy!

5. Explain how you sign "ten dollars."

    _____

    _____

    _____

    _____

10.33 Video Learning Experience

Lessons Six Through Nine Review: Practice Dialogue

Viewing Goal: To improve your comprehension skills by watching a dialogue presented in ASL.

Viewing Instructions: Watch the signed dialogue for comprehension and write a summary of the main points.

_____

_____

_____

_____

_____

10.34 Experiential Activity

Dynamic-Duo Dialogue

Activity Goal: To improve your expressive and receptive ASL skills.

Activity Instructions: Work with a partner to create a dialogue using the vocabulary from Lessons Six, Seven, Eight and Nine. Use ASL (no voices needed!) and be sure each person takes at least four turns.

Be prepared to share your dialogue with the class!

_____

_____

_____

_____

_____

10.35 Video Learning Experience

Lessons Six Thru Nine Review: Practice Story

Viewing Goal: To improve your ASL comprehension skills by watching a story presented in ASL.

Viewing Instructions: Watch the signed story for comprehension and write a summary of the main points.

_____

_____

_____

_____

LESSON TEN

10.36 Homework Assignment

Create-A-Story

Activity Goal: To improve your expressive ASL skills.

Activity Instructions: Create a story using one of the topics below. Be prepared to demonstrate your story for the class!

A. You'll never guess the color of my home!

B. I love school because...

C. Today, at school...

D. If I had a million dollars, I would...

E. I went to the bank, and...

10.37 Post-test Introduction

What Do You Know Now?

Post-test Goal: To assess your mastery of the lesson objectives.

Post-test Introduction: This test has three sections:

Section One: The Comprehension section tests your ability to understand ASL.

Section Two: The Culture and Grammar section tests your knowledge of the material presented in the *Cultural* and *Grammatical Notes*.

Section Three: The Expressive portion tests your ability to use ASL.

Simply follow the instructions for each section.

Good luck!

Lesson 11
PLAYING IN THE PARK

11.2 Homework Review

Create-A-Story

Activity Goal: To show the results of your homework assignment.

Activity Instructions: You will be asked to share the story you created for homework using one of the topics below.

1. You'll never guess the color of my home!
2. I love school because…
3. Today, at school…
4. If I had a million dollars, I would…
5. I went to the bank, and…

While other students perform their stories, pay close attention and practice your comprehension skills! Use ASL to ask questions about signed stories.

11.3 Pretest

What Do You Know?

Pretest Goal: To see how much you already know about what will be taught in this lesson.

Pretest Instructions: Read and answer each question.

1. In ASL, the way signs are used in space often copies the movement of the people and objects involved in the actual events being described.
   A. True
   B. False

2. In an emergency situation, what can medical staff do to improve communication with a patient who is Deaf? Check all that apply:
   A. Look at and speak directly to the Deaf person
   B. Be willing to use gestures
   C. Maintain direct eye contact
   D. Be willing to write or draw pictures

3. During an emergency situation, what are some special concerns a Deaf person might have? Check all that apply:

   A. Will there be a communication problem at the hospital?
   B. Will anyone know Sign Language?
   C. Will there be an interpreter?
   D. Will I have a TV in my room?

4. What issues do you think are important to Deaf people during a medical emergency? Check all that apply:

   A. Getting good medical care
   B. Having communication access
   C. Getting good interpreting services
   D. Getting a color TV in their room

11.4 Lesson Objectives

Planning for Success

Goal: To see what you will learn by the end of this lesson.

Instructions: Read the objectives below. Your instructor will answer any questions you may have.

Upon completing this VideoCourse lesson, you will be able to...

1. Recognize and accurately produce the ASL vocabulary introduced in this and all previous lessons.

2. Identify and explain some of the communication and access issues Deaf people face in a medical emergency.

3. Identify and describe several ways the use of space feature is used in ASL.

11.5 Lesson Focus

Summer Camp Fun!

Activity Goal: To role-play communicating about sports to children who are Deaf.

Activity Instructions: Imagine that you are a camp counselor for a group of children who are Deaf. Your job is to teach the children about the sports and games listed below.

In your group, take turns role-playing a counselor and teaching your campers about the activities. Use signs, mime, and gestures (do not use your voice or write). See if your classmates can guess which activity you are describing.

You are a camp counselor. How would you visually describe...

1. Baseball	4. Running	7. Basketball
2. Tennis	5. Golf	8. Climbing
3. Hiking	6. Fishing	9. A picnic

During this lesson, you will learn the signs for these activities and more. If you ever become a camp counselor, you'll be ready!

Thought/Discussion Questions

1. What are some signs related to sports/games that would have been useful to know for this activity?

   _____

   _____

   _____

   _____

2. How did it feel to be limited in your ability to communicate?

   _____

   _____

   _____

   _____

3. How can Deaf people communicate about sports and games to people who don't sign?

   _____

   _____

   _____

   _____

11.6 Language Learning Instruction

Learning New Signs

Goal: To help you learn new ASL vocabulary.

Instructions: Your instructor will teach you new signs! Watch closely to learn what these signs mean and how they are produced.

In the space below, record any notes to help you remember the signs.

_____

_____

_____

_____

_____

_____

_____

_____

_____

_____

11.7 Video Learning Experience

LESSON ELEVEN

Introduction to New Vocabulary

Viewing Goal: To help you learn new ASL vocabulary.

Viewing Instructions: Watch how Billy produces each sign. Be sure to notice the facial/body expressions. Copy the signs as Billy repeats each one.

Signs representing the following concepts are introduced:

1. TREE	11. SUN	21. GOLF
2. CLIMB+TREE	12. HOT	22. FRISBEE
3. TREES	13. LEAF	23. GAMES
4. FLOWER	14. COOL	24. PLAY
5. SMELL	15. BUTTERFLY	25. PICNIC
6. BLACK+BERRY	16. BASKETBALL	26. WALK
7. BRIDGE	17. BASEBALL	27. RUN
8. WATER	18. BALL	28. FALL-DOWN
9. RIVER	19. TENNIS	
10. GRASS	20. BEAT-ME	

11.8 Experiential Activity

Spot the Sport

Activity Goal: To assist you in recognizing the new ASL vocabulary.

Activity Instructions: You will see signed descriptions of the pictures below. Each of the signed samples will be numbered. Put the number next to the picture that best matches the meaning of each signed description.

11.9 Video Learning Experience

Bravo Family Visit

Viewing Goal: To improve your ASL comprehension skills by watching a Bravo family interaction.

Viewing Instructions: Watch the signed interaction and write a summary of the main points.

_____

_____

_____

_____

_____

_____

_____

_____

11.10 Comprehension Quiz

What Did You Understand?

Quiz Goal: To see how much of the Bravo family interaction you understood.

Quiz Instructions: Read and answer each question below.

1. Anna and Dad discuss how much Lady loves to _____.

   A. Swim

   B. Sleep

   C. Play Frisbee

   D. Play with the ball

2. Anna asks Dad if he wants to play _____.

   A. Frisbee

   B. Tennis

   C. Golf

   D. Football

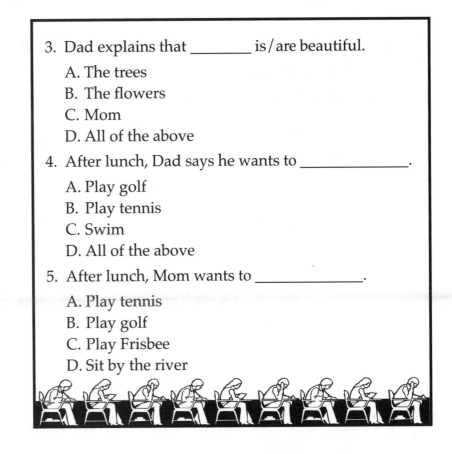

3. Dad explains that _____ is/are beautiful.

    A. The trees
    B. The flowers
    C. Mom
    D. All of the above

4. After lunch, Dad says he wants to _____.

    A. Play golf
    B. Play tennis
    C. Swim
    D. All of the above

5. After lunch, Mom wants to _____.

    A. Play tennis
    B. Play golf
    C. Play Frisbee
    D. Sit by the river

11.11 Language Learning Instruction

Learning New Signs

Goal: To help you learn new ASL vocabulary.

Instructions: Your instructor will teach you new signs! Watch closely to learn what these signs mean and how they are produced.

In the space below, record any notes to help you remember the signs.

_____

_____

_____

_____

_____

_____

_____

_____

_____

_____

11.12 Video Learning Experience

Introduction to New Vocabulary

Viewing Goal: To help you learn new ASL vocabulary.

Viewing Instructions: Watch how Billy produces each sign. Be sure to notice the facial/body expressions. Copy the signs as Billy repeats each one.

Signs representing the following concepts are introduced:

1. MAN
2. WOMAN
3. FISHING
4. PURSE/BAG
5. FIND

11.13 Video Learning Experience

The Frisbee Story

Viewing Goal: To improve your ASL receptive skills.

Viewing Instructions: Watch carefully as Billy signs the *Frisbee Story*. Watch for your new ASL vocabulary and see how the movement of the signs mimics what actually happened to the Frisbee.

Practice signing the following concepts with Billy:

1. The Frisbee was on the ground.
2. Two girls came walking by, found the Frisbee, picked it up, and tossed it back and forth.
3. Their mom came, so the girls had to toss the Frisbee away.
4. There was a woman walking by and the Frisbee landed right in her bag.
5. The woman took the Frisbee out of her bag and tossed it.

6. The Frisbee flew through the air and landed in the river.

7. A man who was fishing thought he'd caught a fish, but it wasn't a fish, it was the Frisbee. He tossed it away and it landed where Scott had left it.

8. Scott thought the Frisbee had stayed in the same place the entire time.

11.14 Video Learning Experience

Grammatical Notes

Viewing Goal: To learn about the grammatical aspects of ASL.

Viewing Instructions: View the *Grammatical Notes* segment carefully for the following:

The Frisbee story demonstrates the use of space grammatical feature of ASL:

A. The movements of ASL signs mimic the actual events being described.

B. Some examples from *The Frisbee Story*:

1. It was established that the Frisbee started its journey lying on the ground.

2. Two girls ran to the Frisbee.

3. The Frisbee was tossed in the direction of the river and it landed on the river. The movement of the signs imitated the movement of the river (bobbing up and down).

4. The Frisbee floated with the current, and the signs indicated the actual movement of the river.

11.15 Experiential Activity

Up, Up, and Away!

Activity Goal: To improve your ASL expressive skills by practicing the use of space feature.

Activity Instructions: Your group is going to create its own Frisbee Story. One person in the group will sign a sentence that tells who or what threw the Frisbee and where it landed. The next person repeats the story and adds another sentence. Pay attention to your classmates so you don't lose the Frisbee!

In the space below, draw a map of your Frisbee's journey. Use arrows to indicate what direction the Frisbee moved.

Hint: You can have your Frisbee go into a tree, into the bathroom, the living-room, the river, the school, etc.

Up, Up, and Away Map

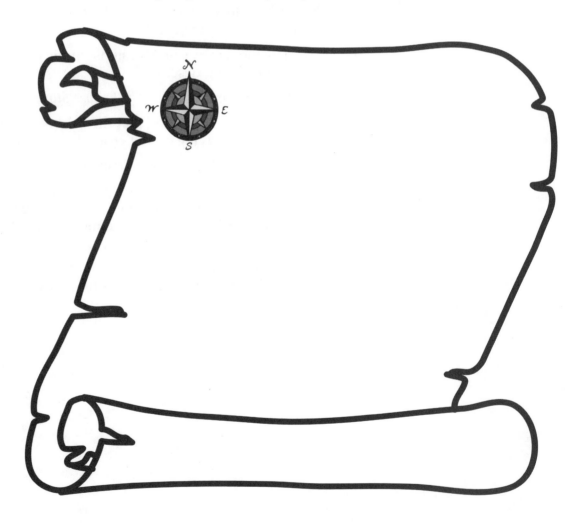

11.16 Video Learning Experience

Bravo Family Visit

Viewing Goal: To improve ASL comprehension skills by watching a Bravo family interaction.

Viewing Instructions: Watch the Bravo family interaction for comprehension. In the space below, write a summary of the main points.

_____

_____

_____

_____

_____

_____

_____

_____

11.17 Video Learning Experience

Cultural Notes

Viewing Goal: To learn about the cultural aspects of ASL.

Viewing Instructions: View the *Cultural Notes* segment carefully for the following:

I. Anyone who has a family member involved in a medical emergency would have many things to think about, including:
    A. Will the person be all right?
    B. Should I call an ambulance?
    C. Will a doctor be available?
    D. Will there be a painful wait?

II. Deaf people have additional concerns, including:
    A. Will I understand all that occurs at the hospital?
    B. Will any of the hospital staff know Sign Language?
    C. Will there be an interpreter available?
    D. In addition to dealing with the emergency, is it my responsibility to teach the hospital staff how to communicate effectively with Deaf people?
    E. Will the medical professionals be sensitive to communication needs?

III. What can medical staff do to facilitate good communication?

    A. Look at and speak directly to the Deaf person.
    B. Be willing to use gestures.
    C. Maintain direct eye contact.
    D. Be willing to write or draw pictures.

11.18 Experiential Activity

It's an Emergency!

Activity Goal: To apply the cultural information you have learned about medical emergencies and Deaf people.

Activity Instructions: Read each situation below and write down any potential problems and the solutions for each.

1. A Deaf four-year-old goes into the hospital for an emergency operation:

    _____
    _____
    _____

2. A Deaf woman goes into labor three weeks early and is admitted to the hospital:

    _____
    _____
    _____

3. A Deaf construction worker is in a work-related accident:

    _____
    _____
    _____

4. A hearing woman is involved in a car accident and wants her Deaf husband to be called:

    _____
    _____
    _____

Thought/Discussion Questions

1. In these situations, how can communication access
   be assured?

   _____

   _____

   _____

2. What are some possible emotional reactions of a
   Deaf person in each of these situations?

   _____

   _____

   _____

3. How might the hearing people in each of these
   situations respond?

   _____

   _____

   _____

11.19 Video Learning Experience

LESSON ELEVEN

Review Session

Viewing Goal: To help you remember how to produce
the signs introduced in this lesson.

Viewing Instructions: Watch this video segment carefully to see how each sign is produced, and take note of
any hints given that might help you remember. You may
want to copy the signs as you watch Billy.

The following are the vocabulary and explanations
offered in this video segment:

TREE	This sign follows the shape of a tree, showing the trunk and all the branches on the top.
TREES	The movement of this sign shows not just one tree, but many TREES.
TALL	This sign follows the shape of a tree trunk. You have to look up because it is TALL!
CLIMB	This sign looks like the action of climbing.
FLOWER	When you pick a flower you might put it by your nose to smell it... so the sign for FLOWER is made near the nose.
BEAUTIFUL	This comes from the idea of a "beautiful face" so these signs are made around the face.

defeat them either way

BLACK+BERRY	As you may remember, the sign for the color BLACK is made on the forehead. The sign for BERRY is made at the tip of your finger. BLACK+BERRY combines these two signs.
BAG/PURSE	This signs shows how you carry a bag or a purse on your arm.
WATER	This is based on the old sign DRINK as in milk, soda, or other beverages. For WATER we use the "W" handshape.
BRIDGE	This sign shows what a bridge looks like, with the support holding up the BRIDGE from underneath.
RIVER	The first part of the sign indicates it is WATER. This is followed by the demonstration of the current or movement of the water.
GRASS	This is an old sign that looks like lying on the ground with the grass in front of your face.
SUN	This sign is made to show the sun as a large circle in the sky. It's like the "eye in the sky."
SUNSHINE	This shows the round shape of the sun, with the fingers as the sun's rays streaming down.
HOT	This sign is made from the mouth, coming from how the warmth of your breath is used to warm your hands.
LEAF	The index finger of one hand is a twig and the other hand is the leaf which falls off and floats to the ground.
COOL	This comes from how you might fan yourself to cool off, or how the wind feels when it is COOL.
BASEBALL	This sign shows how a person holds and uses a bat.
TENNIS	This sign copies how a person actually plays tennis.
GOLF	This sign looks like taking a swing when playing golf.
FRISBEE	This sign shows how you would toss a Frisbee.
GAME	Each hand represents a person. They challenge one another so the hands hit up against each other.
PICNIC	Two signs are demonstrated. One reflects the enthusiasm for going on the outing (rubbing hands together). The other sign depicts the sandwiches you eat on a PICNIC.
WALK	Each hand represents a foot and the movement shows WALKING.
RUN	Do you remember the sign for FAST? Connect your hands and move the index fingers as shown. This sign means to RUN.
FALL	This sign looks like a person falling.

FIND	You're looking for something and you find it.
STAY	This sign tells you to remain. Don't move.
MOVE	You take something from one area and move it to another.
MAN	Remember the sign for BOY? Generally, signs referring to males are produced on or around the forehead.
WOMAN	Generally, signs that indicate female gender are produced on or near the chin.
FISHING	You're holding a long fishing pole... waiting for a bite.

11.20 Video Learning Experience

LESSON ELEVEN

Practice Session: Sentences

Viewing Goal: To improve your comprehension skills by watching sentences presented in ASL.

Viewing Instructions: Watch the signed sentences for comprehension. Remember to watch the face of each signer to see the facial/body expressions and the non-manual grammatical markers as well as the signs.

It is recommended that you copy each signed sentence when it is repeated.

In the space below, record any questions or notes you have regarding the sentences.

_____

_____

_____

_____

_____

_____

_____

_____

_____

_____

_____

11.21 Video Learning Experience

LESSON ELEVEN

Practice Session: Story

Viewing Goal: To improve your comprehension by watching a story presented in ASL.

Viewing Instructions: Watch the signed story for comprehension. In the space below, write a summary of the main points.

_____

_____

_____

_____

_____

_____

_____

_____

_____

11.22 Comprehension Quiz

What Did You Understand?

Quiz Goal: To see how much of the signed story you understood.

Quiz Instructions: Read and answer each question below.

1. Who always won the games?
   A. The woman
   B. The man
   C. The children
   D. The dog

2. The last sport they competed in was _____.
   A. Golf
   B. Frisbee
   C. Running
   D. Fishing

3. The _____ caught the first fish
   A. Boy
   B. Woman
   C. Man
   D. Girl

4. The man caught _____ fish.
   A. Four
   B. Nine
   C. Six
   D. Eight

5. The woman caught _____ fish.
   A. Eight
   B. Seven
   C. Six
   D. Nine

11.23 Experiential Activity

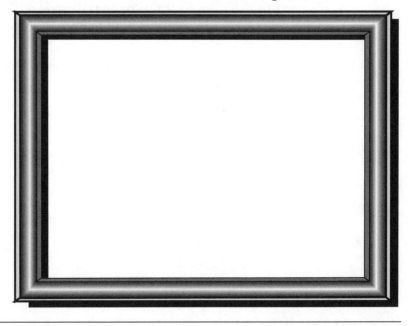

Use of Space Exercise!

Activity Goal: To help you recognize the use of space ASL grammatical feature.

Activity Instructions: Your teacher will replay the video segment *Practice Session: Story*. When you see Billy showing where the woman is or "becoming" the woman in the story, stand up! When you see Billy showing where the man is or "becoming" the man in the story, sit down!

When the story is over, draw a picture of the man and woman fishing. Don't worry about how good your drawing is, just be sure to locate the people in your picture in the same places Billy put them in his "signed picture."

Picture of the man and woman fishing:

11.24 Homework Assignment

A Healthy Visit to the Doctor

Homework Goal: To see how well a medical care facility may be prepared to assist Deaf patients.

Homework Instructions: Visit your own doctor or dentist or a local hospital; walk-in clinic; emergency medical clinic; emergency room; etc. Interview someone about services provided to Deaf individuals.

You may use the following questions during your interview:

1. If a Deaf person came here looking for medical help, how would you communicate with him/her?

2. Has any type of training been provided to your staff to help them meet the needs of Deaf patients?

3. How often have you provided services to Deaf patients?

4. Do you maintain a list of certified/qualified interpreters to contact?

5. How would you obtain the services of Sign Language interpreters?

6. Who would pay for the interpreting services?

7. Do you have the technology to communicate directly?

8. Have you ever received a relay call from a Deaf person?

Use the information from your interview to write a one- to three-page paper describing how prepared this medical care facility is to serve Deaf patients.

11.25 Post-test Introduction

What Do You Know Now?

Post-test Goal: To assess your mastery of the lesson objectives.

Post-test Introduction: This test has three sections.

Section One: The Comprehension section tests your ability to understand ASL.

Section Two: The Culture and Grammar section tests your knowledge of the material presented in the *Cultural* and *Grammatical Notes*.

Section Three: The Expressive portion tests your ability to use ASL.

Simply follow the instructions for each section.

Good luck!

Lesson 12
THE DOCTOR IS IN!

12.2
Homework
Review

A Healthy Visit to the Doctor

Activity Goal: To help you learn from your homework experience.

Activity Instructions: Read and answer the Thought/ Discussion Questions below.

Thought/Discussion Questions

1. Where did you go?

_____
_____
_____
_____

2. Who did you interview?

_____
_____
_____
_____

3. How did people react to your questions?

_____
_____
_____
_____

4. Is there anything you learned that surprised you? If so, what?

_____
_____
_____
_____

---

5. If you were Deaf, would you want to go to this facility during an emergency?

_____

_____

_____

6. What could be done to improve access to the facility you visited?

_____

_____

_____

12.3 Pretest

What Do You Know?

Pretest Goal: To see how much you already know about what will be taught in this lesson.

Pretest Instructions: Read each statement below and determine if it is true or false.

1. In ASL, a lot of information is given through facial expression.
   A. True
   B. False

2. Each ASL sign has only one meaning and one English word to describe it.
   A. True
   B. False

3. ASL uses facial expression the same way English uses adjectives.
   A. True
   B. False

4. All medical facilities are fully accessible to Deaf people.
   A. True
   B. False

5. Medical facilities and personnel are becoming more sensitive to accessibility issues as they relate to the Deaf community.
   A. True
   B. False

12.4 Lesson Objectives

Planning for Success

Goal: To see what you will learn by the end of this lesson.

Instructions: Read the objectives below.

Upon completing this VideoCourse lesson, you will be able to...

1. Recognize and accurately produce the ASL vocabulary introduced in this and all previous lessons.

2. Identify and explain some of the accessibility issues for Deaf people involved in medical emergencies.

3. Explain the role of facial expression in ASL.

4. Accurately recognize and use facial expression within signed communication.

12.5 Lesson Focus

Help! We Need Help!

Activity Goal: To experience a role-play related to medical emergencies when communication is limited.

Activity Instructions: Imagine that you are traveling in a foreign country. The people do not understand English. Your traveling companion falls on the train and hurts her ankle.

How would you communicate the questions or information below without the use of spoken or written communication?

Remember, you can use a variety of methods to communicate, such as gesturing, miming, pointing, etc.

You may make notes of your ideas below:

1. Where is the hospital? _____

2. My friend fell on a train. _____

3. Her ankle hurts very badly. _____

4. Her ankle is swollen. _____

5. Will she need a shot? _____

6. Will you give her medicine? _____

7. Does she need crutches? _____

12.6 Video Learning Experience

Welcome to the Lesson

Viewing Goal: To review how Scott got hurt in the park.

Viewing Instructions: Watch the signed interaction to help you remember how Scott got hurt.

_____

_____

_____

_____

_____

_____

_____

_____

12.7 Language Learning Instruction

Learning New Signs

Goal: To help you learn new ASL vocabulary.

Instructions: Your instructor will teach you new signs! Watch closely to learn what these signs mean and how they are produced.

In the space below, record any notes to help you remember the signs.

_____

_____

_____

_____

_____

_____

_____

_____

_____

_____

12.8 Video Learning Experience

LESSON
TWELVE

Introduction to New Vocabulary

Viewing Goal: To help you learn new ASL vocabulary.

Viewing Instructions: Watch how Billy produces each sign. Be sure to notice the facial/body expressions. Copy the signs as Billy repeats each one.

Signs representing the following concepts are introduced:

1. HOSPITAL
2. DOCTOR
3. NURSE
4. EMERGENCY
5. TAKE-CARE
6. HURT/PAIN
7. ALL-RIGHT/RIGHTS
8. COMMUNICATE
9. WAIT
10. INTERPRET
11. INTERPRETER
12. HOLD/HUG

_____

_____

_____

_____

_____

_____

_____

_____

_____

_____

LESSON TWELVE

12.9 Experiential Activity

Point and Sign

Activity Goal: To improve your ASL receptive and expressive skills.

Activity Instructions: Using the pictures below, follow your teacher's instructions and practice using your new sign vocabulary such as: HOSPITAL; DOCTOR; NURSE; EMERGENCY; HURT; COMMUNICATE; INTERPRET; INTERPRETER; and HOLD.

12.10 Video Learning Experience

LESSON TWELVE

Bravo Family Visit

Viewing Goal: To learn about Deaf people's right to access in the medical setting by watching a Bravo family interaction.

Viewing Instructions: Watch the signed interaction and write a summary of the main points.

_____

_____

_____

_____

_____

_____

_____

12.11 Cultural Quiz

What Did You Learn?

Quiz Goal: To see what cultural aspects of the Bravo family interaction you understood.

Quiz Instructions: Read and answer each question.

1. Why is Mom signing and talking at the same time when she is at the hospital?

   _____

   _____

2. Why is it important for hospitals to know about the rights of the Deaf community *before* a Deaf person visits?

   _____

   _____

3. Why are Deaf people frustrated as they try to fulfill their medical needs?

   _____

   _____

4. Dad served as an advocate for the rights of Deaf people. How did he do this?

   _____

   _____

12.12 Video Learning Experience

Bravo Family Visit

Viewing Goal: To improve ASL comprehension skills by watching a signed interaction.

Viewing Instructions: Watch the signed interaction and write a summary of the main points.

_____

_____

_____

_____

_____

_____

_____

_____

12.13 Video Learning Experience

Bravo Family Visit

Viewing Goal: To improve ASL comprehension skills by watching a signed interaction.

Viewing Instructions: Watch the signed interaction and write a summary of the main points.

_____

_____

_____

_____

_____

_____

_____

_____

12.14 Video Learning Experience

LESSON TWELVE

Grammatical Notes

Viewing Goal: To learn about the grammatical aspects of ASL.

Viewing Instructions: View the *Grammatical Notes* carefully for the following:

I. ASL uses facial expression to complete and enhance the meaning of the signed message:

   A. Dad didn't like filling out the forms so a negative expression was used with the signs:

     <u>eyes rolling and negative expression on face</u>
     PAPER+PAPER+WRITE+WRITE

   B. Billy demonstrates how you can adjust the expression that goes with these same signs to indicate, "happily filling out forms,"

     <u>happy expression on face</u>
     PAPER+PAPER+WRITE+WRITE

II. Expression can change the meaning of signs through degree. Facial expressions serve as the adjectives of the message or sentence. For example, Billy demonstrates how the sign HEADACHE can have three different meanings, depending on the accompanying facial expression:

   A. SMALL HEADACHE

   B. MILD HEADACHE

   C. TERRIBLE HEADACHE

III. Facial expression is a natural part of ASL. A lack of expression can give the signer a wooden or robotic appearance.

12.15 Experiential Activity

What Kind of Face is That?

Activity Goal: To help you recognize the emotions expressed with facial expressions in ASL.

Activity Instructions: You will see several sentences signed in ASL. Watch the facial/body expressions of the signer and circle the adjective that best describes the emotion shown in each signed sentence.

Circle your answers:

1.	Happy	Sad	Bored	Scared
2.	Happy	Sad	Bored	Scared
3.	Happy	Sad	Bored	Scared
4.	Happy	Sad	Bored	Scared
5.	Happy	Sad	Bored	Scared
6.	Happy	Sad	Bored	Scared
7.	Happy	Sad	Bored	Scared
8.	Happy	Sad	Bored	Scared
9.	Happy	Sad	Bored	Scared
10.	Happy	Sad	Bored	Scared

12.16 Video Learning Experience

Bravo Family Visit

Viewing Goal: To learn more about how Deaf people are treated in a medical setting.

Viewing Instructions: Watch the signed interaction and write a summary of the main points.

_____

_____

_____

_____

_____

_____

12.17 Language Learning Instruction

Learning New Signs

Goal: To help you learn new ASL vocabulary.

Instructions: Your instructor will teach you new signs! Watch closely to learn what these signs mean and how they are produced.

In the space below, record any notes to help you remember the signs.

_____

_____

_____

_____

_____

_____

_____

_____

_____

_____

12.18 Video Learning Experience

Introduction to New Vocabulary

Viewing Goal: To help you learn new ASL vocabulary.

Viewing Instructions: Watch how Billy produces each sign. Be sure to notice the facial/body expressions. Copy the signs as Billy repeats each one.

Signs representing the following concepts are introduced:

1. SICK
2. FEEL
3. HOW
4. MEDICINE
5. SNEEZE

6. COLD
7. COUGH
8. SORE-THROAT
9. PILL
10. TEMPERATURE

12.19 Experiential Activity

Diagnosis Dialogue

Activity Goal: To improve your expressive and receptive ASL skills.

Activity Instructions: Work with a partner. Decide who will role-play the doctor and who will role-play the patient.

Using ASL (no voices needed!), create a dialogue in which the patient tells the doctor what is wrong and the doctor makes a diagnosis and treatment recommendation.

Be sure to use your new vocabulary including: SICK; FEEL; HOW; MEDICINE; SNEEZE; COLD; COUGH; SORE-THROAT; PILL; and TEMPERATURE.

Be prepared to share this dialogue with the class!

_____

_____

_____

_____

_____

_____

12.20 Video Learning Experience

Bravo Family Visit

Viewing Goal: To improve your ASL comprehension skills by watching a signed interaction.

Viewing Instructions: Watch the signed interaction and write a summary of the main points.

_____

_____

_____

_____

_____

_____

_____

_____

12.21
Comprehension
Quiz

What Did You Understand?

Quiz Goal: To see how much of the doctor/patient interaction you understood.

Quiz Instructions: Read the questions and circle the best answer.

1. According to Dr. Billy's patient, what is the problem?
   A. He has a fever.
   B. He's nauseated.
   C. He's been sneezing a lot.
   D. He broke his leg.

2. Dr. Billy asks the patient if he's been coughing.
   A. True
   B. False

3. The patient told the doctor he has a sore throat.
   A. True
   B. False

4. The patient is afraid of _____.
   A. The doctor.
   B. Getting a shot.
   C. Missing school.
   D. Losing his teddy bear.

5. The patient was happy because he would miss school, but sad because _____.
   A. He has to stay in the hospital.
   B. He has to take medicine.
   C. He has to get a shot.
   D. He has to rest and can't play.

12.22 Video Learning Experience

Bravo Family Visit

Viewing Goal: To improve ASL comprehension skills by watching a Bravo family interaction.

Viewing Instructions: Watch the signed interaction and be prepared to use ASL to produce a summary of the main points.

_____

_____

_____

_____

_____

_____

_____

_____

12.23 Video Learning Experience

Cultural Notes

Viewing Goal: To help you learn about the cultural aspects of ASL.

Viewing Instructions: View the *Cultural Notes* segment carefully for the following:

I. Awareness and sensitivity about Deaf patient's needs is growing in the medical community.

II. Medical services are becoming more accessible because of:

   A. Deaf people's activism.

   B. State and federal legislation.

   C. People like you learning to interact with the Deaf community.

12.24 Video Learning Experience

Bravo Family Visit

Viewing Goal: To improve ASL comprehension skills by watching a Bravo family interaction.

Viewing Instructions: Watch the signed interaction and be prepared to role-play the "discussion" between Scott and Anna.

Note: Your role-play does not have to be exactly the same as the video, but try to include the main points.

_____

_____

_____

_____

_____

12.25 Video Learning Experience

Review Session

Viewing Goal: To help you remember how to produce the signs introduced in this lesson.

Viewing Instructions: Watch this video segment carefully to see how each sign is produced, and take note of any hints given that might help you remember. You may want to copy the signs as you watch Billy.

The following are the vocabulary and explanations:

HOSPITAL	This sign follows the shape of a medical (Red Cross) symbol on the shoulder.
DOCTOR	This sign shows how a doctor takes a patient's pulse.
NURSE	It's the same idea as DOCTOR, but we use the "N" handshape.
EMERGENCY	This sign shows the flashing lights of an ambulance carrying an injured person.
TAKE-CARE	This sign actually comes from the sign meaning CAREFUL. You are directing that care to another person.
HURT/PAIN	This is like wringing something out, a painful twist in opposite directions. It hurts!
RIGHTS	This is a symbol for the concept RIGHTS. Your facial expression is very important to this sign.

COMMUNICATION	This shows communication going between two people.
INTERPRET	There is a message and you need to express the same meaning in a different language.
INTERPRETER	The AGENT sign is added to the sign for INTERPRET to mean a person who interprets, or an INTERPRETER.
HUG/HOLD	When you hug or hold a person, you do it like this.
UNDERSTAND	It's like a light bulb switches on when you UNDERSTAND.
WAIT	This sign mimics the body's posture and behavior when you are waiting.
FEEL	This is like touching something to see how it feels. You are touching the heart to show your FEELINGS.
SICK	This is like the recent explanation for FEEL. When you are sick, how do you feel in your stomach and your head? Your facial expression must reflect the feeling SICK.
STOMACH	This sign shows where the stomach is.
NAUSEA	Your stomach doesn't feel so good. It is churning and very uncomfortable.
THROW-UP	This sign needs no explanation. It looks like a person THROWING-UP.
TEMPERATURE	This sign reflects the mercury in a thermometer rising when it is hot and falling when it is cold.
INSURANCE	This is a symbol meaning INSURANCE.
SWOLLEN	You hurt yourself and the injury swells. Produce this sign on the body part that was injured.
THROB	This sign's placement, movement, and the accompanying facial expressions should reflect the THROBBING.
AWKWARD/CLUMSY	This shows the clumsy way a duck walks.
BROKE	Something has been broken.
SPRAIN	If a part of the body, for example the joint in your knee, turns the wrong way, it can be SPRAINED.
TWISTED	A joint in the body is TWISTED.
MEDICINE	This sign refers to the action of using a mortar and pestle to grind medication into powder.
SNEEZE	This looks like what most people do when they SNEEZE.
COLD	When you have a cold, you blow your nose again and again.
COUGH	This sign reflects how you look when you COUGH.
PILL	I've already shown you medicine. This shows how you take a PILL.

THROAT	This sign indicates where the throat is located.
SORE-THROAT	The facial expression with this sign conveys that is hurts!
SHOT	This shows how we get shots. There is another sign that shows the plunger pushing medication through the needle.
X-RAY	This sign is often fingerspelled, X-R-A-Y.
BANDAGE	This sign depicts wrapping an injury with a BANDAGE.
PREGNANT	This is what a pregnant woman looks like with a baby inside.
TEASE	It's like an insult. Ouch! When the index finger is bent (hooked), the insult is softer, funny (TEASE). Your facial expression is important to show the intensity of the teasing.

12.26 Experiential Activity

Signs and Origins

Activity Goal: To help you remember how to produce some of the new ASL vocabulary.

Activity Instructions: With a partner, use ASL to discuss the hints and origin information that Billy gave you in the video review session for each of the signs below. These will help you to remember how to make each sign.

Record your notes below.

Sign	Origin/visual hint
1. DOCTOR	_____
2. HURT	_____
3. HUG	_____
4. UNDERSTAND	_____
5. FEEL	_____
6. SICK	_____
7. BROKE	_____
8. SNEEZE	_____
9. PILL	_____
10. PREGNANT	_____

12.27 Video Learning Experience

Practice Session: Sentences

Viewing Goal: To improve your comprehension skills by watching sentences presented in ASL.

Viewing Instructions: Watch the signed sentences for comprehension. Remember to watch the face of each signer to see the facial/body expressions and the non-manual grammatical markers as well as the signs.

It is recommended that you copy each signed sentence when it is repeated.

In the space below, record any questions or notes you have regarding the sentences.

_____

_____

_____

_____

12.28 Video Learning Experience

Practice Session: Story

Viewing Goal: To improve your comprehension by watching a story presented in ASL.

Viewing Instructions: Watch the signed story for comprehension. In the space below, write summary of the main points.

_____

_____

_____

_____

_____

_____

_____

_____

_____

_____

12.29 Comprehension Quiz

What Did You Understand?

Quiz Goal: To see how much of the signed story you understood.

Quiz Instructions: Read and answer each question below.

1. What was the man's name in the story?

   _____

2. How did he get to sleep?

   _____

3. What did he do when he got up?

   _____

4. When he left the house, where did he go?

   _____

5. What did he do while waiting?

   _____

6. What were the doctor's instructions?

   _____

12.30 Experiential Activity

Help! We Need Help Again!

Activity Goal: To experience a role-play related to medical emergencies and apply new communication skills.

Activity Instructions: Imagine that you are traveling with a Deaf friend. Your friend falls on the train and hurts her ankle. Everyone uses ASL.

How would you try to communicate the questions and information below using American Sign Language? Take turns communicating the following information.

1. Where is the hospital?
2. My friend fell on a train.
3. Her ankle hurts very badly.
4. Her ankle is swollen.
5. Will she need a shot?
6. Will you give her medicine?
7. Does she need crutches?

12.31 Homework Assignment

Accessibility Analysis

Homework Goal: To identify accessibility issues when Deaf people are involved in medical emergencies.

Homework Instructions: Watch a TV drama or movie involving a medical setting.

If a Deaf person needed medical care in the situation presented in your TV drama or movie, consider what communication and access problems might exist.

Use the space below to list those problems and recommend what could be done to help medical personnel become more sensitive to the needs of Deaf patients. How could the facilities involved be more accessible to Deaf people?

Accessibility issues: Recommendations:

1. _____   _____

2. _____   _____

3. _____   _____

4. _____   _____

Additional Notes:

_____

_____

_____

_____

_____

12.32 Post-test Introduction

What Do You Know Now?

Post-test Goal: To assess your mastery of the lesson objectives.

Post-test Introduction: This test has three sections:

Section One: The Comprehension section tests your ability to understand ASL.

Section Two: The Culture and Grammar section tests your knowledge of the material presented in the *Cultural* and *Grammatical Notes*.

Section Three: The Expressive portion tests your ability to use ASL.

Simply follow the instructions for each section.

Good luck!

Lesson 13
BUSINESS As UNusual

13.2 Homework Review

Accessibility Analysis

Activity Goal: To show the results of your homework assignment.

Activity Instructions: Use ASL to discuss with your group the communication/access issues you thought might impact a Deaf patient in the medically-oriented television drama or movie you watched. Be sure to share with your group members (using ASL) some of your recommendations for solving these problems.

You can review your notes from *Homework Assignment 12.31.*

Your group should prepare to share its findings with the class.

13.3 Pretest

What Do You Know?

Pretest Goal: To see how much you already know about what will be taught in this lesson.

Pretest Instructions: Read and answer each question.

1. Since a Deaf person can't use the telephone, s/he can't work as a secretary.
   A. True
   B. False

2. Deaf people can't be successful in business because of communication barriers.
   A. True
   B. False

3. Companies that become accessible to Deaf workers are also accessible to Deaf consumers.
   A. True
   B. False

4. What is a relay service?

   A. It is an interpreter referral service.

   B. It is a special machine that helps a Deaf person to use the phone.

   C. It is a service that relays calls between people who are hearing and Deaf.

   D. It is an operator who is Deaf who relays calls to other Deaf people.

5. What type of jobs are available to Deaf people today?

   A. Sign Language teachers and printers.

   B. Photographers, artists, directors, and dancers.

   C. Counselors, secretaries, teachers, lawyers, and doctors.

   D. All of the above.

13.4 Lesson Objectives

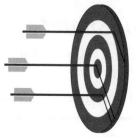

Planning for Success

Goal: To see what you will learn by the end of this lesson.

Instructions: Read the objectives below.

Upon completing this VideoCourse lesson, you will be able to...

1. Recognize and accurately produce the vocabulary introduced in this and all previous lessons.

2. Describe equipment commonly used by Deaf people for gaining access to telecommunication.

3. Describe what a relay service is and how it functions.

4. Identify ways in which the workplace is becoming more accessible to Deaf employees.

5. Accurately produce signs that incorporate numbers.

13.5 Lesson Focus

Help Wanted

Activity Goal: To explore the possibilities and challenges for Deaf people in the workplace.

Activity Instructions: Imagine that you are an employer looking for employees for the jobs described below. You recently interviewed several Deaf people and you were impressed with each person's abilities. You're considering hiring them. You've never had Deaf employees.

Consider modifications to job descriptions or the work environment that might be necessary. How might you make the workplace more accessible to a Deaf employee? Write your ideas below:

JOB TITLE: *Computer Programmer*

MAIN RESPONSIBILITIES:

1) Meet with clients to determine the specifics of their project.

2) Work with team of programmers to design a computer program to meet the client's needs.

3) Check with client(s) throughout process to obtain client feedback.

4) At completion of project, present program and training to client to maximize effective use of program.

Potential communication challenge:	Potential solution:
1. _____	_____
2. _____	_____
3. _____	_____
4. _____	_____

JOB TITLE: Administrative Secretary

MAIN RESPONSIBILITIES:

1) Greet customers as they enter the office.

2) Provide support (such as typing and filing) for staff.

3) Record financial deposits and payables, make bank deposits.

4) At the end of each quarter, write a report regarding the financial status of the company, and present it to the staff.

5) Coordinate company meetings, arranging for food and beverages.

Potential communication challenge:	Potential solution:
1._____	_____
2._____	_____
3._____	_____
4._____	_____

JOB TITLE: Research Librarian

MAIN RESPONSIBILITIES:

1) Meet with students to help them find appropriate research material.

2) Work with teachers and staff members researching information for various school projects.

3) Supervise all research assistants employed by the library.

4) Train students and teachers to use the computerized database.

Potential communication challenge:	Potential solution:
1. _____	_____
2. _____	_____
3. _____	_____
4. _____	_____

13.6 Language Learning Instruction

Learning New Signs

Goal: To help you learn new ASL vocabulary.

Instructions: Your instructor will teach you new signs! Watch closely to learn what these signs mean and how they are produced.

In the space below, record any notes to help you remember the signs.

_____

_____

_____

_____

_____

_____

_____

_____

_____

_____

13.7 Video Learning Experience

LESSON THIRTEEN

Introduction to New Vocabulary

Viewing Goal: To help you learn new ASL vocabulary.

Viewing Instructions: Watch how Billy produces each sign. Be sure to notice the facial/body expressions. Copy the signs as Billy repeats each one.

Signs representing the following concepts are introduced in this video segment.

1. BUSINESS	4. HIRE	7. IDEA
2. COMPANY	5. FIRE	8. EXPLAIN
3. PAY	6. FIRST	9. BORING

13.8 Video Learning Experience

Bravo Family Visit

Viewing Goal: To improve your ASL comprehension skills by watching a Bravo family interaction.

Viewing Instructions: Watch the signed interaction and write a summary of the main points.

_____

_____

_____

_____

_____

_____

_____

_____

13.9 Comprehension Quiz

What Did You Understand?

Quiz Goal: To see how much of the Bravo family interaction you understood.

Quiz Instructions: Read and answer each question.

1. What does Anna ask her mother?

   _____

2. What does Mom invite Anna to do?

   _____

3. Does Anna want to do this?

   _____

4. What does Scott tell Mom NOT to do?

   _____

5. What does Anna plan to do for her first task?

   _____

13.10 Language Learning Instruction

Learning New Signs

Goal: To help you learn new ASL vocabulary.

Instructions: Your instructor will teach you new signs! Watch closely to learn what these signs mean and how they are produced.

In the space below, record any notes to help you remember the signs.

_____

_____

_____

_____

_____

_____

_____

_____

_____

_____

13.11 Video Learning Experience

LESSON THIRTEEN

Introduction to New Vocabulary

Viewing Goal: To help you learn new ASL vocabulary.

Viewing Instructions: Watch how Billy produces each sign. Be sure to notice the facial/body expressions. Copy the signs as Billy repeats each one.

Signs representing the following concepts are introduced in this video segment:

1. WORK
2. OFFICE
3. DESK/TABLE
4. TYPE
5. TYPEWRITER
6. COMPUTER
7. ADVERTISE
8. SECRETARY
9. INTERVIEW
10. SKILL
11. NEED
12. OH-I-SEE
13. ASK-QUESTION

13.12 Video Learning Experience

Bravo Family Visit

Viewing Goal: To improve your ASL comprehension skills by watching a Bravo family interaction.

Viewing Instructions: Watch the signed interaction and write a summary of the main points.

_____

_____

_____

_____

_____

_____

_____

_____

13.13 Comprehension Quiz

What Did You Understand?

Quiz Goal: To see how much of the Bravo family interaction you understood.

Quiz Instructions: Read and answer each question.

1. What does Anna want to know about the computer?

_____

_____

2. What is Mom's computer used for?

_____

_____

3. What does Anna want to do to help Mom?

_____

_____

4. What does Mom do before "hiring" Anna?

_____

_____

5. When Anna answers the phone, who is the caller?

_____

_____

13.14 Language Learning Instruction

Learning New Signs

Goal: To help you learn new ASL vocabulary.

Instructions: Your instructor will teach you new signs! Watch closely to learn what these signs mean and how they are produced.

In the space below, record any notes to help you remember the signs.

_____

_____

_____

_____

_____

_____

_____

_____

_____

_____

13.15 Video Learning Experience

LESSON THIRTEEN

Introduction to New Vocabulary

Viewing Goal: To help you learn new ASL vocabulary.

Viewing Instructions: Watch how Billy produces each sign. Be sure to notice the facial/body expressions. Copy the signs as Billy repeats each one.

Signs representing the following concepts are introduced in this video segment:

1. BOSS
2. LETTER
3. COPY
4. LAZY
5. FILE
6. FILES
7. STAMP
8. ENVELOPE
9. SIGNATURE/SIGN
10. SHELF
11. COMPUTER+PRINTER

13.16 Experiential Activity

Point and Sign

Activity Goal: To improve your ASL receptive and expressive skills.

Activity Instructions: Using the pictures below, follow your teacher's instructions and use your new sign vocabulary, such as: BOSS, LETTER, COPY, FILE, ENVELOPE, SIGNATURE, SHELF, COMPUTER and PRINTER.

13.17 Video Learning Experience

Bravo Family Visit

Viewing Goal: To improve your ASL comprehension skills by watching a Bravo family interaction.

Viewing Instructions: Watch the signed interaction and write a summary of the main points.

_____

_____

_____

_____

_____

_____

_____

_____

13.18
Comprehension Quiz

What Did You Understand?

Quiz Goal: To see how much of the Bravo family interaction you understood.

Quiz Instructions: Read and answer each question.

1. Mom explains that she is Anna's boss.
   A.) True
   B. False

2. What is the first job Mom gives Anna?
   A. Filing
   B. Computer work
   C.) Typing a letter
   D. Going to the post office

3. Who has to sign the letter?
   A. The vice president
   B. The secretary
   C. The president
   D. Anna

4. Mom goes to the post office.
   A. True
   B. False

5. Anna is promoted to what position?
   A. President
   B. Vice president
   C. Secretary
   D. Owner

13.19
Language Learning Instruction

Learning New Signs

Goal: To help you learn new ASL vocabulary.

Instructions: Your instructor will teach you new signs! Watch closely to learn what these signs mean and how they are produced.

In the space below, record any notes to help you remember the signs.

_____

_____

_____

_____

_____

13.20 Video Learning Experience

LESSON THIRTEEN

Introduction to New Vocabulary

Viewing Goal: To help you learn new ASL vocabulary.

Viewing Instructions: Watch how Billy produces each sign. Be sure to notice the facial/body expressions. Copy the signs as Billy signs each one.

Signs representing the following concepts are introduced:

1. PAPER
2. SCISSORS
3. TAPE

4. PAPER+CLIP
5. STAPLER
6. RUBBER-BAND

13.21 Video Learning Experience

LESSON THIRTEEN

Bravo Family Visit

Viewing Goal: To improve ASL comprehension skills by watching a Bravo family interaction.

Viewing Instructions: Watch the signed interaction and write a summary of the main points.

_____

_____

_____

_____

_____

_____

_____

_____

13.22 Comprehension Quiz

What Did You Understand?

Quiz Goal: To see how much of the Bravo family interaction you understood.

Quiz Instructions: Read and answer each question.

1. What does Dad tell Anna he would like to do?

   _____

2. When Dad wants to see Mom, what does Anna ask him?

   _____

3. What does Dad want to do after the women finish working?

   _____

4. What time is it when Mom says work is finished?

   _____

5. How is Anna paid by Mom for her hard work?

   _____

13.23 Video Learning Experience

Review Session

Viewing Goal: To help you remember how to produce the signs introduced in this lesson.

Viewing Instructions: Watch this video segment carefully to see how each sign is produced, and take note of any hints that might help you remember. You may want to copy the signs as you watch Billy.

The following are the vocabulary and explanations:

BUSY — Originally based on the sign for WORK, the sign has become BUSY.

BUSINESS — This sign is based on the sign for BUSY, but it is a little more formal.

COMPANY — Words that are required to be fingerspelled are often abbreviated, because it is faster. We abbreviate company as C-O.

BOSS	This sign is like the epaulets that the commanders wear on the shoulders in the military.
PAY	I am giving money to another person.
HIRE	I am inviting another person to come to work.
FIRE	The fist is a person's body. The head is on top and we cut it off.
FIRST	You have a list of things and this sign represents the first on the list.
EXPLAIN	You have many things and you pull one thing out at a time and define it.
BORING	This is based on the old English phrase, "Put your nose to the grindstone."
OFFICE	This is a compound sign using the signs WORK+ ROOM. The other way is to fingerspell the word, O-F-F-I-C-E.
PROFESSION	There are different fields of work and you concentrate on one area.
CONSULT	This sign shows sending you some of my knowledge.
TYPE	This sign follows the action of how one uses a typewriter.
TYPEWRITER	This is similar to the sign TYPE, but now we are referring to the machine itself.
COMPUTER	This is the same idea as a typewriter but we show the monitor. An older sign depicts the reel-to-reel tape movement.
COMPUTER+PRINTER	This is the sign for PRINT. We add this to the sign for COMPUTER.
LETTER	You write it, fold it, put it in an envelope, and then you put a stamp on it.
SIGNATURE/SIGN	You have a piece of paper that you put (SIGN) your name on.
ENVELOPE	This shows the shape of the envelope and how you seal it.
STAMP	This sign represents putting the stamp on an envelope.
SEND	You have just finished the letter, you put a stamp on it then you mail it.
DESK	This sign reflects the flat surface of the DESK.
DRAWER	This sign shows how you open a DRAWER.
SHELF	This sign shows what a shelf, or shelves, look like.
COPY	This sign shows how an image is copied from a page.
FILE	There is a folder and documents are put in or stored in the folder.

LESSON THIRTEEN

FILES	The sign for FILE is repeated several times.
LAZY	When you're lazy your body slumps. We use the "L" handshape.
PRESIDENT	This is like the bull who is the leader of the herd. We show the horns of the bull to make the sign for PRESIDENT.
VICE-PRESIDENT	This is an abbreviation instead of fingerspelling VICE PRESIDENT (V-P). Also, the signing space is a little lower than that for PRESIDENT.
POST-OFFICE	An abbreviation for P-O-S-T O-F-F-I-C-E is P-O.
SCISSORS	This sign mirrors how scissors are used.
STAPLE/STAPLER	This sign shows how you use a STAPLER.
CHECK	This sign shows the shape of a CHECK.
TAPE	This is based on how one uses TAPE.
PAPER+CLIP	You have already learned the sign for PAPER, the other hand shows the CLIP on the paper.
RUBBER-BAND	A rubber band is circular and very elastic.
MEETING	This sign represents a group of people together discussing something.
EARN	There is a pile of money here and I collect it.
SCHEDULE	This is like the grid of days and weeks shown on a calendar.
APPOINTMENT	You are holding or reserving a time. It is like having a calendar and holding on to one day.
ASSISTANT	The one hand represents the boss, the other hand is below, supporting the boss.
ASK	This sign often expresses a request. Another way is with the index finger making the shape of a question mark.
INTERVIEW	This sign reflects a dialogue between two people. We use the "I" handshape.
SKILL	This sign is based on the old sign for GREASE. A professional knows what to do in their field. They are "smooth as oil."
NEED	This is a symbolic representation. There are several meanings to this sign but the facial expression tells you this is NEED.
OH-I-SEE	Hearing people have vocal responses like hmmm, oh, really, and ahhh. Deaf people use the "Y" handshape and the specific feeling is added through facial expression. OH-I-SEE.

promotion move ↑ level.

*SEcretary.
advertising*

13.24 Video Learning Experience

LESSON THIRTEEN

Practice Session: Sentences

Viewing Goal: To improve your comprehension skills by watching sentences presented in ASL.

Viewing Instructions: Watch the signed sentences for comprehension. Remember to watch the face of each signer to see the facial/body expressions and the non-manual grammatical markers as well as the signs.

It is recommended that you copy each signed sentence when it is repeated.

In the space below, record any questions or notes you have regarding the sentences.

_____

_____

_____

_____

_____

13.25 Experiential Activity

Create-A-Sentence

Activity Goal: To improve your expressive and comprehension skills by creating ASL sentences.

Activity Instructions: With a partner, take turns creating sentences in ASL. Choose at least one vocabulary item from Column A and at least one from Column B to form each sentence.

Column A	Column B
JOB	SIGNATURE
INTERVIEW	BOSS
SKILL	NEED
LAZY	SEND
TYPEWRITER	ASK-QUESTION
LETTER	FIRE
FILE	DRAWER
CHECK	COMPUTER

13.26 Video Learning Experience

Cultural Notes

Viewing Goal: To learn about the cultural aspects of ASL.

Viewing Instructions: View the *Cultural Notes* segment carefully for the following:

I. Telephones and their impact on employment for Deaf people:

  A. Deaf people have been denied jobs or discriminated against because the job required the use of a telephone.

  B. Modern technologies, including those listed below, have improved this situation.

    1. Internet and email
    2. Videophones (VP) and Video Relay Services (VRS)
    3. Computer technology

II. Video Relay Service:

  A. Facilitates communication between a person with a video phone (VP) or a video camera/computer and a person using a voice-only telephone.

    1. A VRS interpreter facilitates communication between the d/Deaf and hearing people involved in the call.
    2. The VRS service is needed and used by both hearing and Deaf people.

  B. VRS helps make more jobs accessible to Deaf people.

III. As technology continues to develop, the barriers to communication are decreasing.

13.27 Video Learning Experience

Grammatical Notes

Viewing Goal: To learn about the grammatical aspects of ASL.

Viewing Instructions: View the *Grammatical Notes* for the following:

Combining numbers and signs:

  A. Numbers can be incorporated with pronouns:

    1. TWO-OF-US uses the number TWO sign.
    2. FOUR-OF-US uses the number FOUR sign.

  B. Numbers can be incorporated with time:

    1. ONE-MONTH, TWO-MONTH, etc.
    2. ONE-WEEK, TWO-WEEK, etc.

13.28
Experiential
Activity

Name the Number

Activity Goal: To identify the meaning of sentences including a number incorporated with signs, as taught in this lesson.

Activity Instructions: You will see five signed sentences. Each sentence will be signed twice. Circle the picture that best illustrates the meaning of each sentence.

13.29 Video Learning Experience

LESSON THIRTEEN

Practice Session: Story

Viewing Goal: To improve your comprehension by watching a story presented in ASL.

Viewing Instructions: Watch the signed story for comprehension. In the space below, write a summary of the main points.

_____

_____

_____

_____

_____

_____

_____

_____

13.30 Comprehension Quiz

What Did You Understand?

Quiz Goal: To see how much of the signed story you understood.

Quiz Instructions: Read and answer each question.

1. Where does Anna work?

   _____

2. Who does Anna interview?

   _____

3. What kind of worker is the new employee?

   _____

4. What does the new employee do instead of work?

   _____

5. What does the new employee do to Anna?

   _____

6. What does the new employee demand of Anna?

   _____

7. What does Anna do instead?

   _____

13.31 Homework Assignment

A Day at the Office

Homework Goal: To improve your expressive skills.

Homework Instructions: Create a story about a day at the office using the pictures below. The story must include at least eight of the ASL vocabulary introduced in this lesson and use at least three numbers incorporated into signs as presented in the *Grammatical Notes* segment. Be prepared to share your story with the class.

13.32 Post-test Introduction

What Do You Know Now?

Post-test Goal: To assess your mastery of the lesson objectives.

Post-test Introduction: This test has three sections:

Section One: The Comprehension section tests your ability to understand ASL.

Section Two: The Culture and Grammar section tests your knowledge of the material presented in the *Cultural* and *Grammatical Notes*.

Section Three: The Expressive portion tests your ability to use ASL.

Simply follow the instructions for each section.

Good luck!

Lesson 14
LET'S GO CLOTHES SHOPPING!

14.2 Homework Review

A Day at the Office

Activity Goal: To show the results of your homework assignment.

Activity Instructions: Take turns in your group signing the story *A Day at the Office* assigned for homework in Lesson Thirteen. You may look at the pictures in activity 13.31 to help you.

When it is your turn to sign your story, remember to include at least eight of the work-related signs you learned in Lesson Thirteen, and at least three examples of incorporating numbers with signs, as instructed in the *Grammatical Notes*.

When your classmates are signing, pay close attention and practice your ASL comprehension skills. Use ASL to ask questions about their stories.

Be prepared to sign your story to the class.

14.3 Pretest

What Do You Know?

Pretest Goal: To see how much you already know about what will be taught in this lesson.

Pretest Instructions: Read and answer each question.

1. Most Deaf children are born to hearing parents.
   A. True *80-90%*
   B. False

2. Many hearing parents with Deaf children never learn to sign.
   A. True *3%*
   B. False

3. Parents must consider the individual needs of their child before making important decisions about communication.
   A. True
   B. False

ultimate words nue

LESSON
FOURTEEN

4. If a child learns to sign, that means s/he will never learn to talk.
   A. True
   B. False

5. The term "classifiers" refers to:
   A. A class of people who use ASL.
   B. A class of Deaf children who misbehave.
   C. A class of objects represented by a certain hand shape.
   D. A class of students that urgently want to learn ASL.

6. Which of these vehicles cannot be signed with the "3" handshape?
   A. Car
   B. Motorcycle
   C. Boat
   D. Airplane *flying plane*

7. What numbers can be incorporated into classifiers? (Check all that apply.)
   _✓_ A. 1
   _✓_ B. 2
   _✓_ C. 3
   _✓_ D. 4

14.4 Lesson Objectives

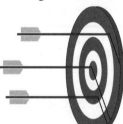

Planning for Success

Goal: To see what you will learn by the end of this lesson.

Instructions: Read the objectives below.

Upon completing this VideoCourse lesson, you will be able to...

1. Recognize and accurately produce the ASL vocabulary introduced in this and all previous lessons.

2. Identify some of the key issues parents face in making decisions regarding communication when raising a Deaf child.

3. Identify some of the communication options available to Deaf children.

4. Define "classifiers" and recognize their use in signed communication.

5. Accurately produce and use classifiers within the context of signed communication.

14.5 Lesson Focus

What Are They Wearing?

Activity Goal: To find out what clothing signs you know (and which you need to learn).

Activity Instructions: You will see several signed descriptions of people and what they are wearing. Watch carefully, and for each description, circle the correct picture below.

1. A.   B.   C.

2. A.   B.   C.

3. A.   B.   C.

4. A.   B.   C.

LESSON FOURTEEN

Thought/Discussion Questions

1. What are some signs related to clothing that would have been useful to know during this activity?

_____

_____

2. How did it feel to be limited in your ability to understand the signed descriptions?

_____

_____

3. What are some techniques that Deaf people could use in describing people and their clothes to people who do not sign?

_____

_____

14.6 Language Learning Instruction

Learning New Signs

Goal: To help you learn new ASL vocabulary.

Instructions: Your instructor will teach you new signs! Watch closely to learn what these signs mean and how they are produced.

In the space below, record any notes to help you remember the signs.

_____

_____

_____

_____

_____

_____

_____

_____

14.7 Video Learning Experience

Introduction to New Vocabulary

Viewing Goal: To help you learn the new ASL vocabulary.

Viewing Instructions: Watch how Billy produces each sign. Be sure to notice the facial/body expressions. Copy the signs as Billy repeats each one.

Signs representing the following concepts are introduced in this video segment:

1. CLOTHES
2. STORE
3. SHOPPING/BUYING
4. TOWEL
5. LIKE
6. DON'T-LIKE
7. TALL
8. TWO-OF-US
9. THREE-OF-US
10. PANTS
11. SHIRT/SWEATER
12. TIE
13. HAT

14.8 Experiential Activity

Point and Sign

Activity Goal: To help you recognize and produce the new ASL vocabulary.

Activity Instructions: Using ASL, discuss the pictures below with your group. Use your new ASL vocabulary such as: CLOTHES; TWO-OF-US; STORE; THREE-OF-US; SHOPPING/BUYING; PANTS; TOWEL; SHIRT/ SWEATER; LIKE; TIE; DON'T-LIKE; HAT; and TALL.

14.9 Video Learning Experience

Bravo Family Visit

Viewing Goal: To improve your ASL comprehension by watching a Bravo family interaction.

Viewing Instructions: Watch the signed interaction and write a summary of the main points.

_____

_____

_____

_____

_____

_____

_____

_____

14.10 Comprehension Quiz

What Did You Understand?

Quiz Goal: To see how much of the Bravo family interaction you understood.

Quiz Instructions: Read and answer each question.

1. When Scott first meets Tommy, what does he ask?
   A. "How old are you?"
   B. "Do you have a sister?"
   C. "Where is your father?"
   D. "Are you Deaf?"

2. After Tommy fingerspelled his name, what did Scott do?
   A. Gave him a new name.
   B. Gave him a name sign.
   C. Told him his fingerspelling was too slow.
   D. Told him he was too tall.

3. What does Scott ask Tommy?
   A. If he wants to buy pants.
   B. If he wants to buy a mask.
   C. If he wants to walk around the store together.
   D. If he wants Anna as a girlfriend.

4. What are some of the signs Scott taught Tommy?
   A. MASK, PANTS, and SISTER
   B. PANTS, SHIRT, SOCKS, and SHOES
   C. DEAF, HEARING, SISTER, and BROTHER
   D. SCARE, PETER PAN, CLOTHES, and COAT

5. What are some of the signs Dad taught Tommy's father?
   A. HAT, TIE, and GLOVES
   B. MIRROR, OVERALLS, and HAT
   C. EXPENSIVE, BUY, and DRESS
   D. MONEY, SON, and FAMILY

14.11 Language Learning Instruction

Learning New Signs

Goal: To help you learn new ASL vocabulary.

Instructions: Your instructor will teach you new signs! Watch closely to learn what these signs mean and how they are produced.

In the space below, record any notes to help you remember the signs.

_____

_____

_____

_____

_____

_____

_____

_____

_____

_____

14.12 Video Learning Experience

Introduction to New Vocabulary

Viewing Goal: To help you learn new ASL vocabulary.

Viewing Instructions: Watch how Billy produces each sign. Be sure to notice the facial/body expressions. Copy the signs as Billy repeats each one.

Signs representing the following concepts are introduced in this video segment:

1. DRESS
2. SKIRT
3. COAT
4. SOCKS
5. SHOES
6. BACKPACK
7. PURSE
8. PRICE/COST
9. BIG/LARGE
10. CUTE
11. FANCY
12. COMFORTABLE
13. LUCKY
14. DINNER
15. LOVE-IT

14.13 Video Learning Experience

Bravo Family Visit

Viewing Goal: To improve your ASL comprehension skills by watching a Bravo family interaction.

Viewing Instructions: Watch the signed interaction and write a summary of the main points.

_____

_____

_____

_____

_____

_____

_____

_____

14.14 Video Learning Experience

Cultural Notes

Viewing Goal: To learn about the cultural aspects of ASL.

Viewing Instructions: View the *Cultural Notes* carefully for the following:

I. Most Deaf children are born to hearing parents.

   A. Many hearing parents know little or no Sign Language.

   B. They have had little, if any, contact with other Deaf people.

   C. It is hard for parents to know what to do, in deciding the best way to raise their Deaf child.

   D. Many professionals like doctors, counselors, teachers, disagree on which communication method is best.

      1. For example, some doctors tell parents that if their child learns Sign Language they will never learn to speak.

      2. Some doctors advocate strongly that hearing aids and speech training must be used.

      3. Some doctors advise the use of Sign Language and natural language development through visual means.

II. Sign Enhancers believes that there is not one right way to raise all Deaf children.

A. Each child's individual needs must be identified and addressed.

B. Parents have the responsibility to research the various methods and options.

C. Parents should weigh the positive and negative aspects of each option before a decision can be reached.

III. Another important point is that parents must keep a close watch on their child as the child grows.

A. Parents need to monitor the child's response.

B. Parents must remain flexible, making changes that best suit their child. Billy shares, "For me personally, as a Deaf person, I greatly value American Sign Language. It has helped me connect to the world in ways which helped me find out more about who I am and how I fit in.

"My parents are hearing and they do not use Sign Language. I attended an oral, mainstream program where Sign Language wasn't used.

"If I could live my life over and change anything I wanted, I would make it so American Sign Language was introduced to me at a very young age. I know I would have been happier."

IV. The most important thing is communication.

A. Tommy and his parents discovered the excitement of learning American Sign Language.

B. By expanding communication options, it could change their lives.

C. You are never too old - nor is it ever too late - to learn a new language.

14.15 Experiential Activity

Panel Discussion

Activity Goal: To give you the opportunity to meet Deaf people and learn firsthand about their personal communication options and preferences.

Activity Instructions: Your instructor will invite some Deaf people to have a panel discussion. Use the space on the following page for notes. You may also want to write down questions you have for the speakers or for your instructor.

Panel Discussion Notes:

_____

_____

_____

_____

_____

_____

_____

Thought/Discussion Questions

1. What did you learn from this panel?

_____

_____

2. How did each of the panel members feel about their communication options?

_____

_____

3. Did this panel change your opinion about any particular communication option(s)?

_____

_____

14.16 Video Learning Experience

Bravo Family Visit

Viewing Goal: To improve your ASL comprehension by watching a Bravo family interaction.

Viewing Instructions: Watch the signed interaction and write a summary of the main points.

_____

_____

_____

_____

_____

_____

14.17 Comprehension Quiz

What Did You Understand?

Quiz Goal: To see how much of the Bravo family interaction you understood.

Quiz Instructions: Read and answer each question.

1. Anna likes the dress because Tommy said he liked it.

   A. True
   B. False

2. What does Scott tell Anna about the coat she tried on?

   A. "It looks too big on you."
   B. "You look warm."
   C. "It looks good on you."
   D. "You look cold."

3. What does Tommy ask Anna?

   A. "Do you like backpacks?"
   B. "Do you like purses?"
   C. "Why don't you carry a purse?"
   D. "Do you want to go hiking?"

4. What does Scott tell Mom when they meet again?

   A. "Tommy is my new friend."
   B. "Tommy doesn't know how to sign."
   C. "We've been teaching Tommy signs!"
   D. "Anna likes Tommy!"

5. Why does Scott say he and Anna are lucky?

   A. Because they bought socks and a coat for Anna.
   B. Because they have a new friend
   C. Because they know how to sign.
   D. Because their parents sign.

6. What does Tommy's father tell him when he says he loves Sign Language

   A. "It's too late to learn now."
   B. "I love you."
   C. "I love Sign Language, too."
   D. "I love this store."

LESSON FOURTEEN

14.18 Video Learning Experience

LESSON FOURTEEN

Review Session

Viewing Goal: To help you remember how to produce the signs introduced in this lesson.

Viewing Instructions: Watch this video segment carefully to see how each sign is made, and take note of any hints given to help you remember. You may want to copy the signs as you watch Billy.

The following are the vocabulary and explanations offered in this video segment:

CLOTHES	This sign represents the clothes covering the body.
STORE	The sign for SELL moves once. For a place that has many things to sell, the sign moves twice. It is a STORE.
SHOPPING/BUYING	The sign for BUY moves once. When you buy a number of things, moving the sign several times, you are SHOPPING.
TOWEL	You take a towel and dry your back. This sign shows that action.
LIKE	Your body is drawn to something you see, it attracts you.
DON'T-LIKE	This is the opposite of LIKE. You don't want it near you, so you turn it away.
TALL	Billy demonstrates two signs. One sign represents the concept TALL. The other sign specifically shows the top of a person's head.
TWO-OF-US	This sign points to a person and the signer.
THREE-OF-US	This indicates the signer and two others.
PANTS	Billy shows two ways to sign PANTS. The first clearly shows putting pants on. The other sign shows the shape and design.
SHIRT	This shows how a shirt is worn on the body.
TIE	This sign shows what a tie looks like and how it is worn.
HAT	This shows something on the top of the head.
DRESS	This shows the shape and location of a DRESS.
SKIRT	This sign shows the skirt starting from the waist and indicates the shape and location of a SKIRT.
COAT	The movement of this sign indicates the action of putting on a coat with thick, heavy material.

SOCKS	Billy demonstrates two signs for SOCKS. In the first sign, the fingers are the legs. The second sign shows one hand as the foot and the other hand as putting the sock over the foot.
SHOES	This sign represents the hard covering on your feet.
BACKPACK	This sign shows how the straps attach the BACKPACK.
PURSE	How do you use a purse? You carry it by the handle or you can hang it from your arm.
PRICE/COST	This is like the old hand-held machine used to place labels and tags on items, indicating the price of an item.
LARGE/BIG	This shows that something is LARGE.
CUTE	What does an adult will do to a cute child? Pinch the child's chin.
FANCY	When something is really fine, it is FANCY.
EXPENSIVE	Make the sign for MONEY and then show that there is a pile of it.
COMFORTABLE	This represents what your hands do when sitting back comfortably.
LUCKY	This is a symbolic representation.
DINNER	This is a compound sign indicating when you eat dinner, EAT+NIGHT
LOVE-IT	You kiss the back of your hand, meaning you really like or cherish something.

14.19 Experiential Activity

Wacky Wardrobe Stories

Viewing Goal: To improve your ASL skills with signs related to clothing.

Viewing Instructions: Your teacher will divide your class into pairs. Take a few minutes to study the pictures below. Each partner will sign a *Wacky Wardrobe Story*, using as many of the pictures below as possible. Circle the pictures you plan to use when you sign your story.

When you and your partner are ready, Partner A will sign your story while Partner B watches and places an X by each picture s/he recognizes in the story.

When the story is over, Partner B should sign to Partner A the numbers of all the pictures used in the story. Partner A will check to see if Partner B got them all!

Repeat this activity, switching roles.

14.20 Video Learning Experience

LESSON FOURTEEN

Grammatical Notes

Viewing Goal: To learn about the grammatical aspects of ASL.

Viewing Instructions: View the *Grammatical Notes* segment carefully for the following:

  I. Classifiers (abbreviated as CL):

    A. There are many classifiers, which show a *class* of objects/people. For example, the 1-handshape can represent or become a number of cylinder-like objects, such as a person, pole, tree, pencil, etc.

B. It is possible - with the addition of facial expressions and body language - to express different ideas.
For example, PERSON-WALKING can be modified to be a casual walk, a determined walk, a hurried walk, or even a sad walk.

C. We can use the other hand (with 1-handshape) to show two people greeting each other and walking on (or perhaps, intentionally avoiding each other).

II. Classifiers with the 2-handshape:

A. Upright, it can mean TWO-PEOPLE-WALKING.

B. Turned upside down, it can represent the legs of a person or animal:

JUMPING
FALLING
WALKING-QUIETLY

III. Classifiers with the 3- handshape can represent THREE-PEOPLE-WALKING. In the video, Billy shows the children using this classifier.

IV. Classifiers with the 4-handshape can be used to represent a number of people standing and waiting in a line.

V. Classifiers with V-handshapes can represent the four legs of an animal:

RUNNING (galloping)
KICKING (front legs)
KICKING (back legs)
LYING-DOWN

VI. Classifiers with the 3-handshape (thumb facing up) can be used to refer to vehicles such as:

CAR   TRAIN
TRUCK MOTORCYCLE
BUS   BICYCLE
BOAT

Note: Because of its location and movement, AIRPLANE's classifier is different. It is demonstrated on the DVD.

14.21 Experiential Activity

Classy Classifiers

Viewing Goal: To improve your skills with classifiers.

Viewing Instructions: View the signed sentences and select the answer that best matches the meaning of each.

1. A The man walked to the store.
   B. The woman walked to the store.
   C. The man drove to the store.
   D. The man walked fast to the store.

2. A. The father hurried home.
   B. The mother drove fast.
   C. The mother hurried to the house.
   D. The mother asked where the house was.

3. A. The man took a train.
   B. The man drove up the hill.
   C. The boy rode his bike up a hill.
   D. The man drove down the hill.

4. A. The car went fast!
   B. The man ran fast!
   C. The horse ran fast!
   D. The dog ran fast!

5. A. The children ran through the store.
   B. The mother and father strolled through the store.
   C. The children walked slowly through the school.
   D. The mother and father hurried through the store.

6. A. The car drove on the street.
   B. The airplane took off.
   C. The airplane landed safely.
   D. The boat rode on the water.

7. A. The two of us took a walk together.
   B. The three of us took a walk together.
   C. The four of us took a walk together.
   D. The five of us took a walk together.

8. A. Dad hurried to the bathroom.
   B. Dad carefully walked to the kitchen.
   C. Dad jumped up and down on the bed.
   D. Dad tiptoed through the bedroom.

9. A. The students waited in line for the food.
   B. The eight of us walked together.
   C. The line moved fast.
   D. The students wentto class.

10. A. Sara fell.
    B. Sara was so happy, she jumped up and down!
    C. Sally was so happy, she jumped up and down!
    D. Sally skipped around the house.

14.22 Video Learning Experience

Practice Session: Sentences

Viewing Goal: To improve your ASL comprehension skills by watching signed sentences.

Viewing Instructions: Watch the signed sentences for comprehension. Remember to watch the face of each signer to see the facial/body expressions and the non-manual grammatical markers as well as the signs.

It is recommended that you copy each signed sentence when it is repeated.

In the space below, record any questions or notes you have regarding the sentences.

_____

_____

_____

_____

_____

14.23 Experiential Activity

You're Going to Wear That!?!

Activity Goal: To improve your expressive and receptive ASL skills with clothing signs.

Activity Instructions: A volunteer will go to the front of the room, where there will be a pile of clothing and accessories. The volunteer will select a classmate and use ASL to tell that person what to wear from the pile. When the classmate is "dressed," s/he will select another student to "dress," and so on.

Be creative! Choose the wildest combination of colors and styles you can find! Try to make the person you dress look outrageous.

The class will vote to see who was dressed the wildest.

14.24 Video Learning Experience

Practice Session: Story

Viewing Goal: To improve your ASL comprehension by watching a story presented in ASL.

Viewing Instructions: Watch the signed story for comprehension. In the space below, write a summary of the main points.

_____

_____

_____

_____

14.25 Comprehension Quiz

What Did You Understand?

Quiz Goal: To see how much of the signed story you understood.

Quiz Instructions: Read and answer each question.

1. What was the girl's name in the story?
   A. Amy
   B. Angie
   C. Anna
   D. Alice

2. What did the girl's mother want to buy?
   A. A purple skirt with a pink blouse.
   B. A blue skirt with a purple blouse.
   C. Blue pants, a shirt, and a backpack.
   D. A pink skirt, blouse, and purse.

3. What did the girl want to buy?
   A. A purple skirt with a pink blouse.
   B. A blue skirt with a purple blouse.
   C. Blue pants, a shirt, and a backpack.
   D. All of the above.

4. What choice did the girl's mother give her?

   _____

   _____

5. What did the girl decide to buy?

   _____

LESSON FOURTEEN

14.26 Homework Assignment

ASL SitCom

Homework Goal: To provide you with the opportunity to create and perform a short situation comedy using the ASL vocabulary related to clothes shopping.

Homework Instructions: Work with your group to create and perform a skit entitled, *The Hilarious Clothing Store Adventure!*

Your group's skit and all preparation work is to be done using ASL (no voices needed!). Every student in the group must have a part and actively participate in the creation and performance of the skit.

Be sure to use at least ten new ASL vocabulary from this lesson and at least five classifiers in your skit. Be prepared to perform your skit for the rest of the class. Who knows - it might even end up on television!

Have fun... and please pass the popcorn!

14.27 Post-test Introduction

What Do You Know Now?

Post-test Goal: To assess your mastery of the lesson objectives.

Post-test Introduction: This test has three sections:

Section One: The Comprehension section tests your ability to understand ASL.

Section Two: The Culture and Grammar section tests your knowledge of the material presented in the *Cultural* and *Grammatical Notes*.

Section Three: The Expressive portion tests your ability to use ASL.

Simply follow the instructions for each section.

Good luck!

Lesson 15
REVIEW & PRACTICE SESSION

15.2 Homework Review

ASL SitCom!

Activity Goal: To perform the skits you prepared for homework.

Activity Instructions: Your group will have the chance to perform your skit, *The Hilarious Clothing Store Adventure!*

Remember, every student in each group must have a part and actively participate in the performance.

Be sure to use at least ten of the ASL vocabulary learned in Lesson Fourteen and at least five classifiers.

Smile... you might be on camera!

15.3 Lesson Objectives

Planning for Success

Goal: To see what you will learn by the end of this lesson.

Instructions: Read the objectives below.

Upon completing this VideoCourse lesson, you will be able to...

1. Recognize and accurately produce the ASL vocabulary introduced in Lessons Eleven, Twelve, Thirteen, and Fourteen.

2. Demonstrate knowledge of the cultural information presented in Lessons Eleven, Twelve, Thirteen, and Fourteen.

3. Recognize and apply the grammatical features presented in Lessons Eleven, Twelve, Thirteen, and Fourteen.

4. Accurately use the ASL vocabulary and grammatical features presented in Lessons Eleven, Twelve, Thirteen, and Fourteen in sentences, dialogues and stories.

15.4 Video Learning Experience

LESSON FIFTEEN

Lesson Introduction

Viewing Goal: To help you prepare for this review session.

Viewing Instructions: Billy will explain what you can expect from this *Review & Practice Session*.

Pay attention to what he is signing, but also notice *how* he expresses these ideas with facial/body expression, non-manual grammatical markers and use of space. Perhaps you will learn a few more signs!

In the space below, write any notes or questions you may have.

_____

_____

_____

_____

15.5 Experiential Activity

Sport Stories

Activity Goal: To help you remember the ASL vocabulary learned in Lesson Eleven.

Activity Instructions: In your group, choose one of the topics below and create an ASL story. Everyone must sign part of the story! Use as many of the ASL vocabulary that you learned in Lesson Eleven as possible (see the Illustration Section for Lesson Eleven vocabulary).

Have fun... and be prepared to sign your story for the class!

Sport Story Topics:

1. The day we played basketball in the park...
2. How the golfer fell in the river...
3. Fishing from the bridge...
4. The basketball game that was interrupted by a butterfly...

In the space below, write notes to help you develop and remember the story.

_____

_____

_____

_____

LESSON FIFTEEN

15.6 Video Learning Experience

LESSON FIFTEEN

Lesson Eleven Review: Vocabulary

Viewing Goal: To help you review the ASL vocabulary from Lesson Eleven.

Viewing Instructions: Watch the Lesson Eleven vocabulary review. Raise your hand if there is a sign you do not remember.

Signs representing the following concepts are reviewed:

1.	TREE	17.	COOL
2.	TREES	18.	BASEBALL
3.	TALL	19.	TENNIS
4.	CLIMB	20.	GOLF
5.	FLOWER	21.	FRISBEE
6.	PRETTY/BEAUTIFUL	22.	GAME
7.	BLACK+BERRY	23.	PICNIC
8.	BAG/PURSE	24.	WALK
9.	WATER	25.	RUN
10.	BRIDGE	26.	FALL
11.	RIVER	27.	FIND
12.	GRASS	28.	STAY
13.	SUN	29.	MOVE
14.	SUN+SHINE	30.	MAN
15.	HOT	31.	WOMAN
16.	LEAF	32.	FISHING

_____

_____

_____

_____

_____

_____

_____

_____

_____

15.7 Video Learning Experience

Lesson Eleven Review: Sentences

Viewing Goal: To improve your comprehension skills by watching sentences presented in ASL.

Viewing Instructions: Watch the signed sentences for comprehension. Remember to watch the face of each signer to see the facial/body expressions and the non-manual grammatical markers as well as the signs.

It is recommended that you copy each signed sentence when it is repeated.

In the space below, record questions or notes regarding the sentences.

_____

_____

_____

_____

_____

_____

_____

_____

15.8 Video Learning Experience

Lesson Eleven Review: Practice Dialogue

Viewing Goal: To improve your comprehension skills by watching a dialogue presented in ASL.

Viewing Instructions: Watch the signed dialogue for comprehension and write a summary in the space provided.

_____

_____

_____

_____

_____

_____

_____

_____

15.9 Experiential Activity

Dynamic-Duo Dialogue

Activity Goal: To improve your expressive and receptive ASL skills.

Activity Instructions: Work with a partner to create a dialogue using the Lesson Eleven vocabulary (see activity 15.6 for the vocabulary list). Use ASL (no voices needed!) and be sure each person takes at least five turns signing. Be prepared to share your dialogue with the class!

In the space below, record ideas or notes you have regarding the dialogue.

_____

_____

_____

_____

15.10 Video Learning Experience

LESSON FIFTEEN

Bravo Family Revisited

Viewing Goal: To reinforce your ASL comprehension skills by reviewing a Bravo family interaction from Lesson Eleven.

Viewing Instructions: Watch the *Bravo Family Revisited* for review. Be prepared to use ASL to summarize what happened in this video segment.

15.11 Experiential Activity

Medical Drama

Activity Goal: To help you improve your skills with the ASL vocabulary learned in Lesson Twelve.

Activity Instructions: Work with your group to create and perform a skit involving the medical setting. Use as many of the ASL signs you learned in Lesson Twelve as possible (see the Illustration Section for Lesson Twelve vocabulary). Everyone in the group needs to have an active role in the drama!

Be prepared to perform your *Medical Drama* for the class!

LESSON FIFTEEN

15.12 Video Learning Experience

Lesson Twelve Review: Vocabulary

Viewing Goal: To help you review the ASL vocabulary from Lesson Twelve.

Viewing Instructions: Watch the Lesson Twelve vocabulary review. Raise your hand if there is a sign you do not remember, and your instructor will help you.

Signs representing the following concepts are reviewed in this video segment:

1. HOSPITAL
2. DOCTOR
3. NURSE
4. EMERGENCY
5. TAKE-CARE
6. HURT/PAIN
7. ALL-RIGHT/RIGHTS
8. COMMUNICATE
9. WAIT
10. INTERPRET
11. INTERPRETER
12. HOLD/HUG
13. SICK
14. FEEL
15. HOW
16. MEDICINE
17. SNEEZE
18. COLD
19. COUGH
20. SORE-THROAT
21. PILL
22. TEMPERATURE

15.13 Video Learning Experience

Lesson Twelve Review: Sentences

Viewing Goal: To improve your comprehension skills by watching sentences presented in ASL.

Viewing Instructions: Watch the signed sentences for comprehension. Remember to watch the face of each signer to see the facial/body epressions and the non-manual grammatical markers as well as the signs.

It is recommended that you copy each signed sentence when it is repeated.

In the space below, record any questions or notes you have regarding the sentences.

_____

_____

_____

_____

_____

_____

15.14 Video Learning Experience

Lesson Twelve Review: Practice Dialogue

Viewing Goal: To improve your comprehension skills by watching a dialogue presented in ASL.

Viewing Instructions: Watch the signed dialogue for comprehension and answer the questions below.

1. What does Scott tell Anna at the beginning of the dialogue?
   _____
   _____

2. Anna tells Scott that she is not going to school. What is the first reason she gives him?
   _____
   _____

3. According to Scott, how will Mom know she is faking?
   _____
   _____

4. What is the second symptom Anna tells Scott about?
   _____
   _____

5. When Anna tells Scott that she has a headache, how does he respond?
   _____
   _____

6. In the end, does Anna decide to go to school or stay home?
   _____
   _____

15.15 Experiential Activity

Dynamic-Duo Dialogue

Activity Goal: To improve your expressive and receptive ASL skills.

Activity Instructions: Work with a partner to create a dialogue using the Lesson Twelve vocabulary (see the Illustration Section for Lesson Twelve vocabulary). Use ASL (no voices needed!) and be sure each person takes at least five turns signing.

Be prepared to share your dialogue with the class!

In the space below, record ideas or notes you have regarding the dialogue.

_____

_____

_____

_____

_____

15.16 Video Learning Experience

LESSON FIFTEEN

Bravo Family Revisited

Viewing Goal: To improve your ASL comprehension skills by reviewing a Bravo family interaction.

Viewing Instructions: Watch the *Bravo Family Revisited* for review and write a summary in the space below.

_____

_____

_____

_____

_____

15.17
Experiential
Activity

Matchmaker

Activity Goal: To help you remember some of the ASL vocabulary learned in Lesson Thirteen.

Activity Instructions: Look at the illustrations below. Draw a line from the illustration of the sign to the picture that best matches its meaning.

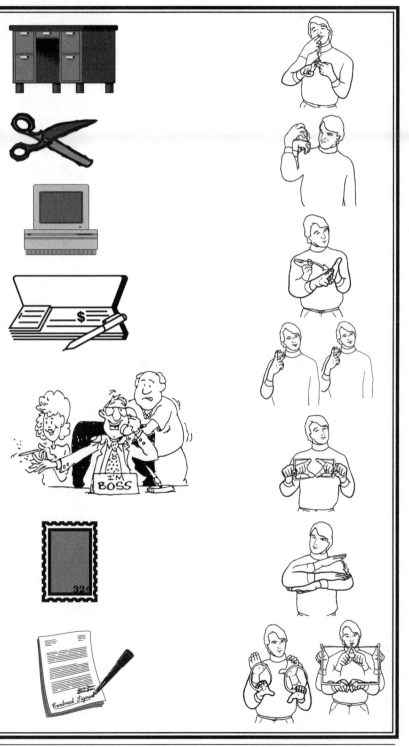

15.18 Video Learning Experience

Lesson Thirteen Review: Vocabulary

Viewing Goal: To help you review the ASL vocabulary from Lesson Thirteen.

Viewing Instructions: Watch the Lesson Thirteen vocabulary review while you copy the signs.

Signs representing the following concepts are reviewed:

1. BUSINESS	14. TYPEWRITER	27. FILE
2. COMPANY	15. COMPUTER	28. FILES
3. PAY	16. ADVERTISE	29. STAMP
4. HIRE	17. SECRETARY	30. ENVELOPE
5. FIRE	18. INTERVIEW	31. SIGNATURE/SIGN
6. FIRST	19. SKILL	32. SHELF
7. IDEA	20. NEED	33. COMPUTER+PRINTER
8. EXPLAIN	21. OH-I-SEE	34. PAPER
9. BORING	22. ASK-QUESTION	35. SCISSORS
10. WORK	23. BOSS	36. TAPE
11. OFFICE	24. LETTER	37. PAPER+CLIP
12. DESK/TABLE	25. COPY	38. STAPLER
13. TYPE	26. LAZY	39. RUBBER-BAND

15.19 Video Learning Experience

Lesson Thirteen Review: Sentences

Viewing Goal: To improve your comprehension skills by watching sentences presented in ASL.

Viewing Instructions: Watch the signed sentences for comprehension. Remember to watch the face of each signer to see the facial/body expressions and the non-manual grammatical markers as well as the signs.

It is recommended that you copy each signed sentence when it is repeated.

In the space below, record any questions or notes you have regarding the sentences.

_____

_____

_____

_____

_____

15.20 Video Learning Experience

Lesson Thirteen Review: Practice Dialogue

Viewing Goal: To improve your comprehension skills by watching a dialogue presented in ASL.

Viewing Instructions: Watch the signed dialogue for comprehension and write a summary in the space provided.

_____

_____

_____

_____

_____

_____

_____

15.21 Experiential Activity

Dynamic-Duo Dialogue

Activity Goal: To improve your expressive and receptive ASL skills.

Activity Instructions: Work with a partner to create a dialogue using the Lesson Thirteen vocabulary (see the Illustration Section for Lesson Thirteen vocabulary). Use ASL (no voices needed!) and be sure each person takes at least five turns.

Be prepared to share your dialogue with the class!

In the space below, record ideas or notes you have regarding the dialogue.

_____

_____

_____

_____

_____

_____

_____

_____

15.22 Video Learning Experience

LESSON FIFTEEN

Bravo Family Revisited

Viewing Goal: To reinforce your ASL comprehension skills by reviewing a Bravo family interaction from Lesson Thirteen.

Viewing Instructions: Watch the signed interaction carefully for review. Be prepared to role-play this interaction with your classmates. Each person in your group will take on the character of one of the Bravo family members.

_____

_____

_____

_____

15.23 Experiential Activity

Point and Sign

Activity Goal: To help you review the ASL vocabulary learned in Lesson Fourteen.

Activity Instructions: Using the pictures below, follow your teacher's instructions and practice using the Lesson Fourteen sign vocabulary.

15.24 Video Learning Experience

Lesson Fourteen Review: Vocabulary

Viewing Goal: To help you review the ASL vocabulary from Lesson Fourteen.

Viewing Instructions: Watch the Lesson Fourteen vocabulary review while you copy the signs. Raise your hand if there is a sign you do not recognize, and your instructor will help you.

Signs representing the following concepts are reviewed in this video segment:

1. CLOTHES	15. SKIRT
2. STORE	16. COAT
3. SHOPPING/BUYING	17. SOCKS
4. TOWEL	18. SHOES
5. LIKE	19. BACKPACK
6. DON'T-LIKE	20. PURSE
7. TALL	21. PRICE/COST
8. TWO-OF-US	22. BIG/LARGE
9. THREE-OF-US	23. CUTE
10. PANTS	24. FANCY
11. SHIRT/SWEATER	25. COMFORTABLE
12. TIE	26. LUCKY
13. HAT	27. DINNER
14. DRESS	28. LOVE-IT

15.25 Video Learning Experience

Lesson Fourteen Review: Sentences

Viewing Goal: To improve your comprehension skills by watching sentences presented in ASL.

Viewing Instructions: Watch the signed sentences for comprehension. Remember to watch the face of each signer to see the facial/body expressions and the non-manual grammatical markers as well as the signs. It is recommended that you copy each signed sentence when it is repeated.

In the space below, record any questions or notes you have regarding the sentences.

_____

_____

_____

_____

15.26 Video Learning Experience

Bravo Family Revisited

Viewing Goal: To improve your ASL comprehension skills by reviewing a Bravo family interaction.

Viewing Instructions: Watch the *Bravo Family Revisited* for review and write a summary in the space below.

_____

_____

_____

_____

15.27 Experiential Activity

Pictures in the Air

Activity Goal: To improve your expressive and comprehension skills.

Activity Instructions: Your group will be assigned one of the pictures below. Work with your group to create a skit in ASL (no voice!) about your picture. Your group will have time to prepare and practice your skit and then show it to the whole class.

15.28 Video Learning Experience

Lessons Eleven Thru Fourteen Review: Grammatical Notes

Viewing Goal: To help you apply the ASL grammatical aspects presented in Lessons Eleven, Twelve, Thirteen and Fourteen.

Viewing Instructions: Answer the questions below to see how well you remember these grammatical aspects. When you are finished, watch the video. Billy will provide the answers so you can see how well you did.

---

1. What is the grammatical feature of ASL that allows the signs to mirror actual events, following the same direction of movement, location, and relative size of objects?
   A. Use of signs
   B. Use of space
   C. Use of adjectives
   D. Use of facial expression

2. Signs and numbers are sometimes combined and used together. Can you think of two examples showing a number incorporated within a sign?
   A. _____
   B. _____

3. What is the grammatical feature which prevents signing from looking boring?
   _____
   _____

4. How would you explain what a classifier is?
   _____
   _____

15.29 Video Learning Experience

Lessons Eleven Thru Fourteen Review: Cultural Notes

Viewing Goal: To review the cultural aspects presented in Lessons Eleven, Twelve, Thirteen, and Fourteen.

Viewing Instructions: Answer the questions on the following page to see how well you remember these cultural aspects of ASL. When you are finished, watch the video. Billy will provide you with the answers to correct your work.

---

1. What are some issues and concerns a Deaf person faces in a medical emergency? (Check all that apply.)
   __ A. Will the medical services be accessible?
   __ B. Can the hospital staff sign?
   __ C. Will there be an interpreter available?
   __ D. Will I be able to get my medical needs met?

2. There are actually federal laws requiring equal accessibility and communication at hospitals receiving federal funding.
   A. True
   B. False

3. Unfortunately, the laws are not always followed.
   A. True
   B. False

4. Today however, the world is changing. More people relearning ASL, and learning about Deaf culture.
   A. True
   B. False

5. What are two benefits of making businesses accessible to Deaf people?
   A. _____
   B. _____

6. The majority of Deaf children have hearing parents.
   A. True
   B. False

7. Parents need to focus on their child's unique needs when making choices regarding communication options.
   A. True
   B. False

8. When communicating with a Deaf person, what can you do to be sensitive to that person's needs? (Circle all that apply):
   A. Address the person directly.
   B. Maintain eye contact.
   C. Write or draw if needed.
   D. Speak loudly and slowly.

15.30 Video Learning Experience

Lessons Eleven Thru Fourteen Review: Practice Story

Viewing Goal: To improve your ASL comprehension skills by watching a story presented in ASL.

Viewing Instructions: Watch the signed story for comprehension. Be prepared to use ASL to retell the story.

15.31 Video Learning Experience

Congratulations, You Did It!

Viewing Goal: To receive well-deserved congratulations!

Viewing Instructions: Sign Enhancers wants to congratulate you on a job well done! Watch the signed message for encouragement to continue improving your skills.

15.32 Post-test Introduction

What Do You Know Now?

Post-test Goal: To assess your mastery of the lesson objectives.

Post-test Introduction: This test has three sections:

Section One: The Comprehension section tests your ability to understand ASL.

Section Two: The Culture and Grammar section tests your knowledge of the material presented in the *Cultural* and *Grammatical Notes*.

Section Three: The Expressive portion tests your ability to use ASL.

Simply follow the instructions for each section.

Good luck!

Sign Illustration Index

SIGN ILLUSTRATIONS

Sign Illustration Index

SIGN ILLUSTRATIONS

Sign Illustration Index

SIGN ILLUSTRATIONS

Sign Illustration Index

SIGN
ILLUSTRATIONS

LESSON ONE: ASL VOCABULARY

ALMOST

BABY

BED

BREAKFAST

BRUSH-TEETH

CHILDREN

COFFEE

DAUGHTER

DEAF

DOG

SIGN ILLUSTRATIONS

LESSON ONE: ASL VOCABULARY

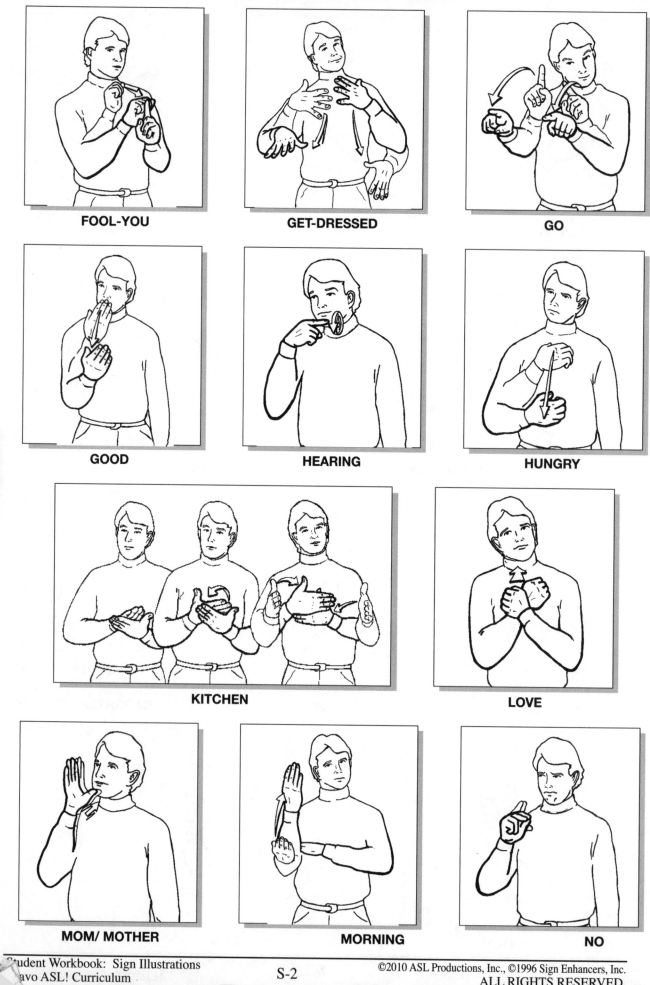

FOOL-YOU

GET-DRESSED

GO

GOOD

HEARING

HUNGRY

KITCHEN

LOVE

MOM/ MOTHER

MORNING

NO

SIGN ILLUSTRATIONS

LESSON ONE: ASL VOCABULARY

PAST/ BEFORE

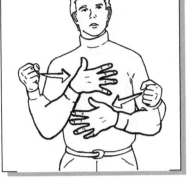

SCARED/ AFRAID

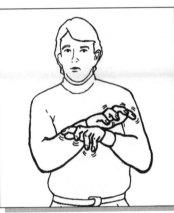

SCHOOL

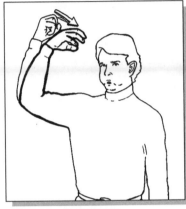

SHOWER

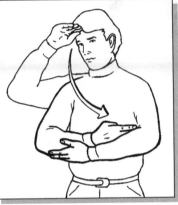

SON

SPIDER

THANK-YOU

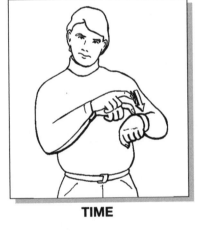

TIME

TOILET/ BATHROOM

WAKE-UP

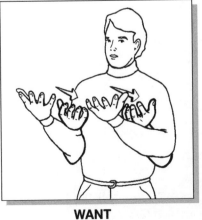

WANT

SIGN
ILLUSTRATIONS

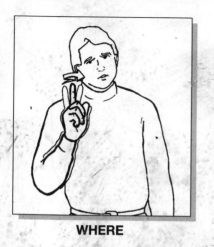

WHERE

WHICH

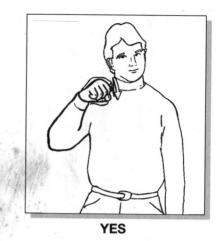

YES

LESSON TWO: ASL VOCABULARY

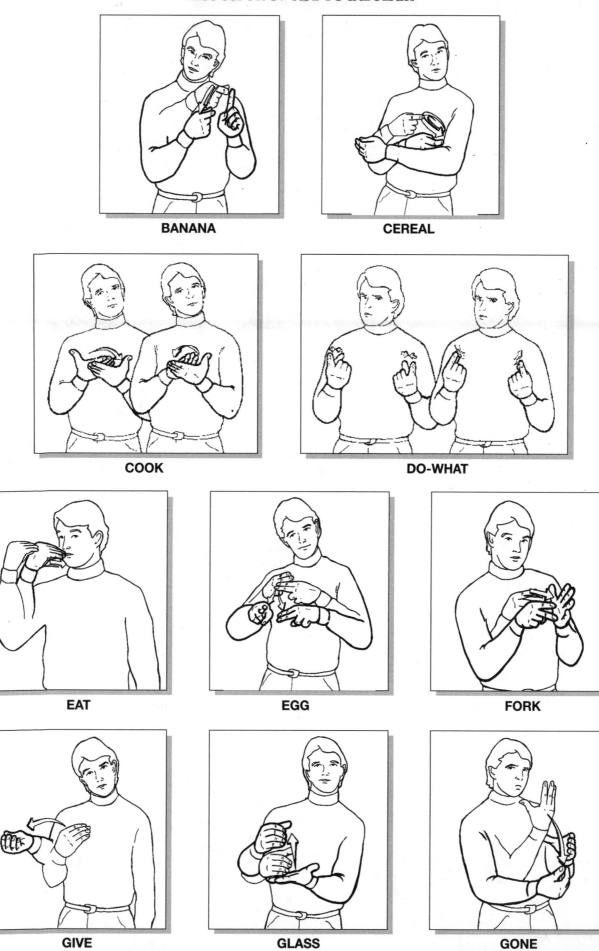

BANANA

CEREAL

COOK

DO-WHAT

EAT

EGG

FORK

GIVE

GLASS

GONE

LESSON TWO: ASL VOCABULARY

HELP

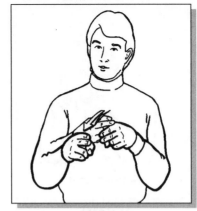

KNIFE

MILK

MY-TURN

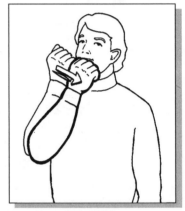

NAPKIN

ONE

ORANGE-JUICE

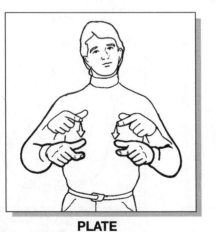

PLATE

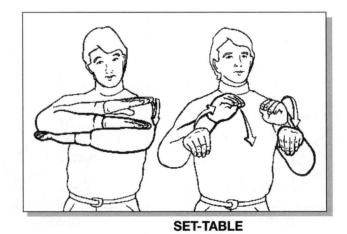

SET-TABLE

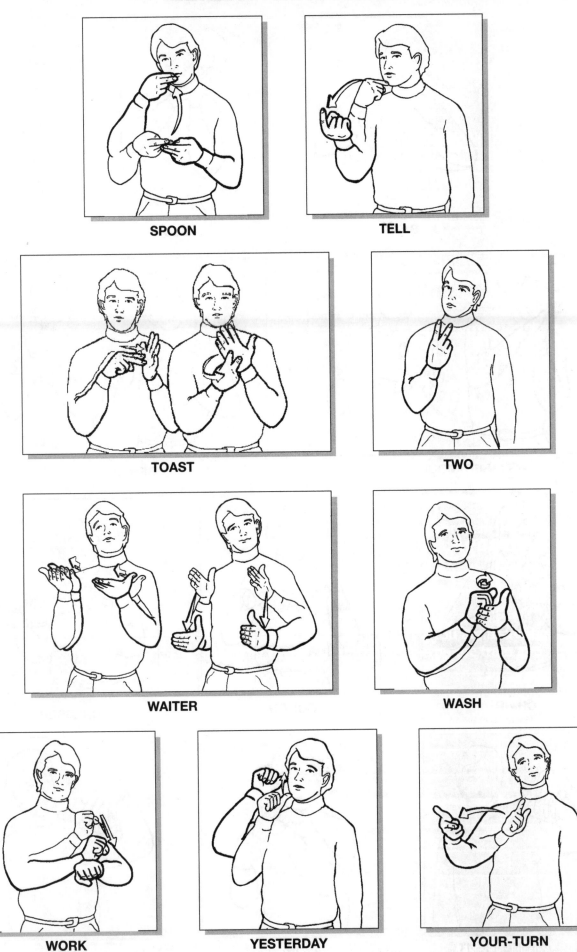

SPOON

TELL

TOAST

TWO

WAITER

WASH

WORK

YESTERDAY

YOUR-TURN

SIGN
ILLUSTRATIONS

LESSON THREE: ASL VOCABULARY

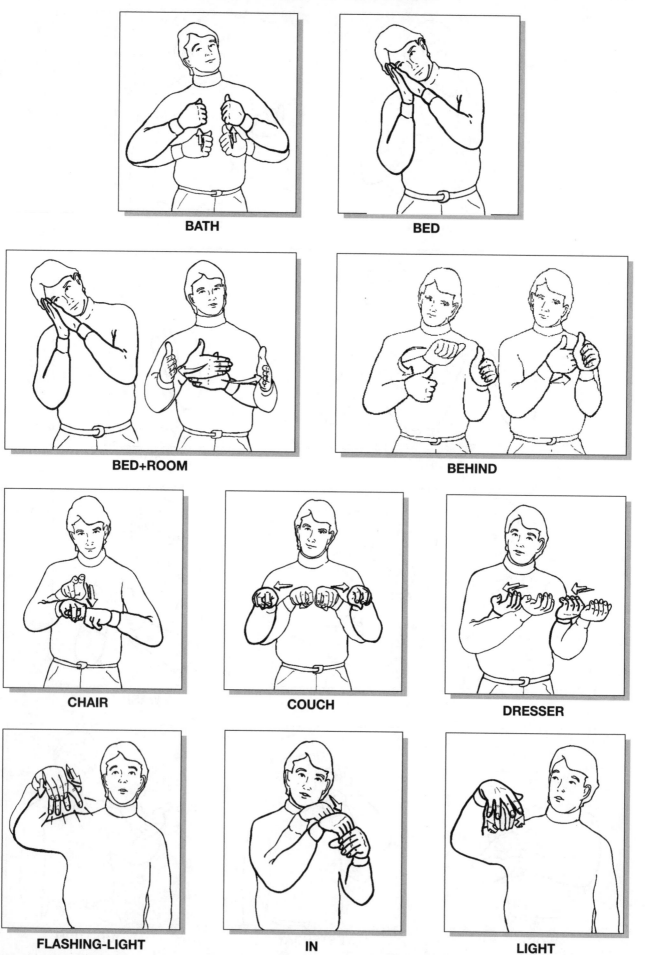

BATH

BED

BED+ROOM

BEHIND

CHAIR

COUCH

DRESSER

FLASHING-LIGHT

IN

LIGHT

LESSON THREE: ASL VOCABULARY

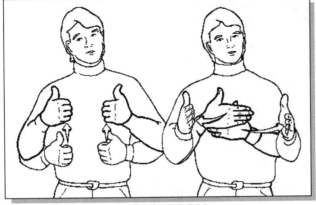

LIVING+ROOM

ON

OVEN

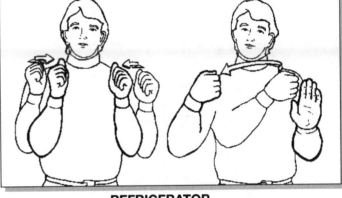

REFRIGERATOR

REMOTE-CONTROL

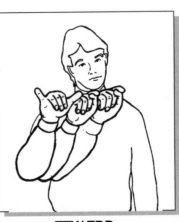

SINK

TELEPHONE

TTY/ TDD

SIGN ILLUSTRATIONS

T.V.

UNDER

UPSTAIRS

what?
where?
whose?

PREPOSITION
under
in
behind
on

SIGN ILLUSTRATIONS

LESSON FOUR: ASL VOCABULARY

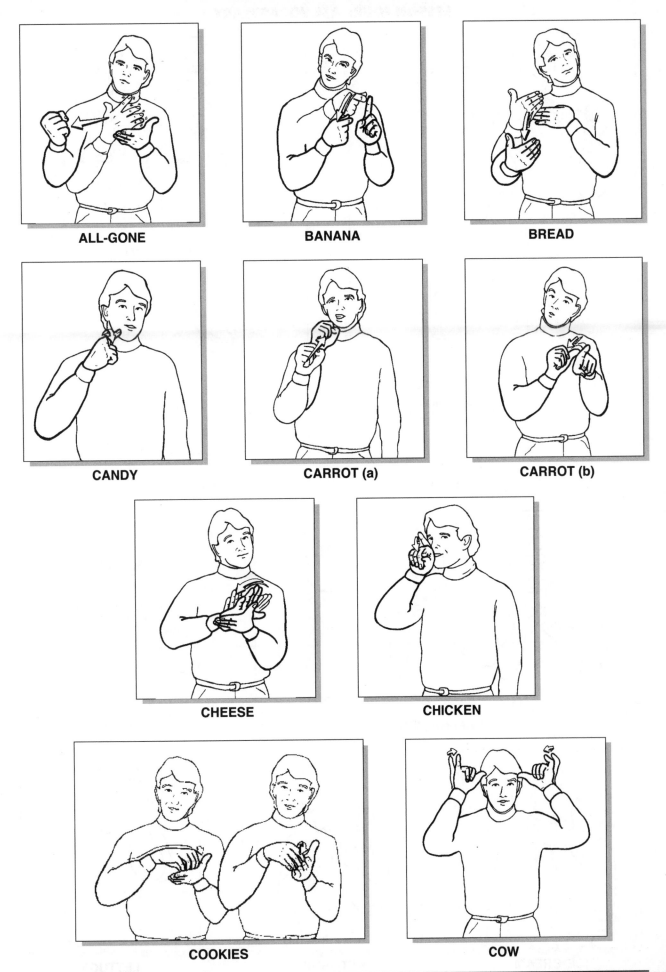

ALL-GONE

BANANA

BREAD

CANDY

CARROT (a)

CARROT (b)

CHEESE

CHICKEN

COOKIES

COW

SIGN
ILLUSTRATIONS

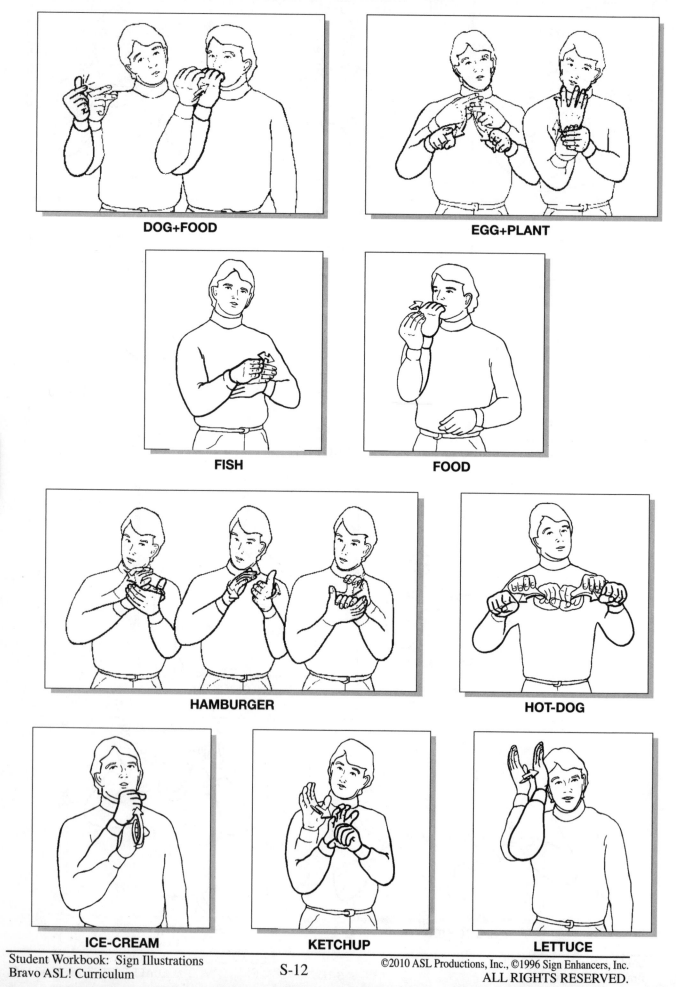

DOG+FOOD

EGG+PLANT

FISH

FOOD

HAMBURGER

HOT-DOG

ICE-CREAM

KETCHUP

LETTUCE

SIGN ILLUSTRATIONS

LESSON FOUR: ASL VOCABULARY

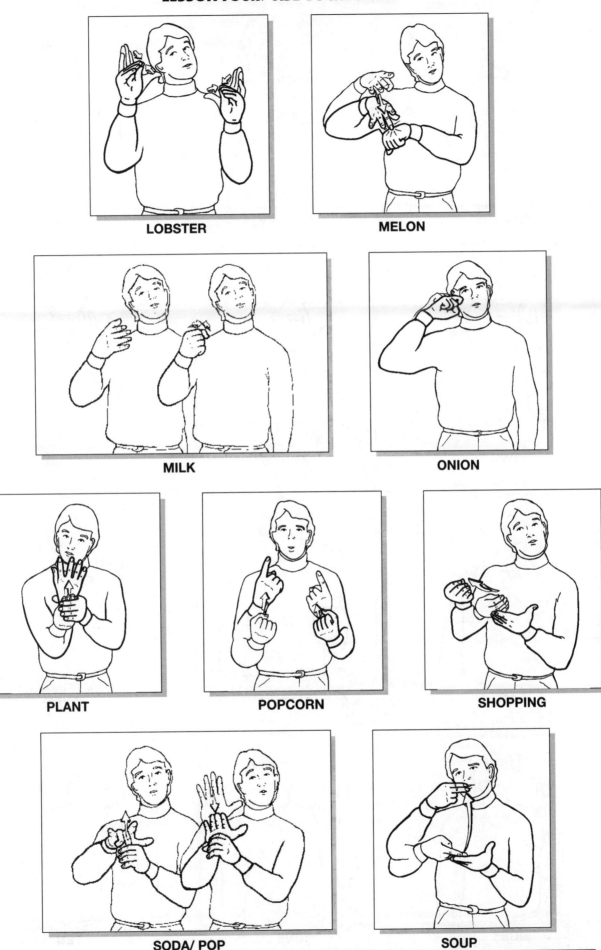

LOBSTER

MELON

MILK

ONION

PLANT

POPCORN

SHOPPING

SODA/ POP

SOUP

SIGN ILLUSTRATIONS

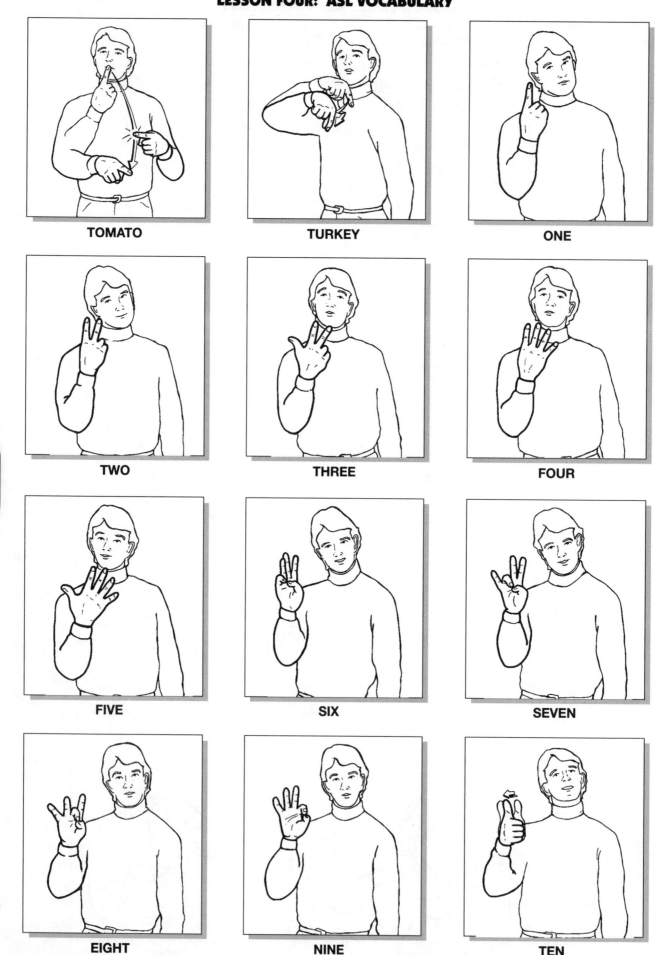

TOMATO

TURKEY

ONE

TWO

THREE

FOUR

FIVE

SIX

SEVEN

EIGHT

NINE

TEN

SIGN ILLUSTRATIONS

LESSON SIX: ASL VOCABULARY

BLACK

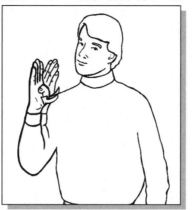

BLUE

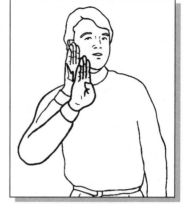

BROWN

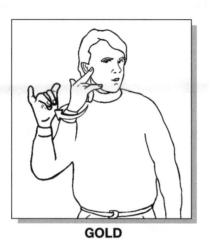

GOLD

GREEN

ORANGE

PINK

PURPLE

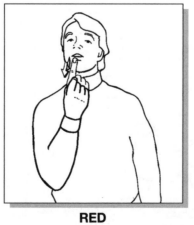

RED

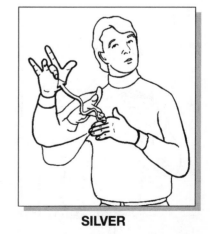

SILVER

TAN

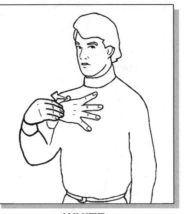

WHITE

YELLOW

A

B

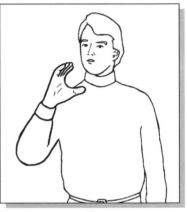

C

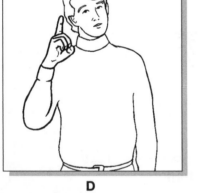

D

E

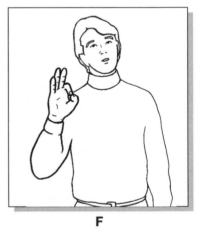

F

G

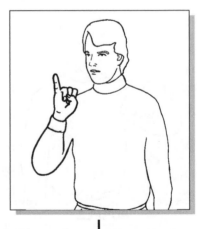

H

I

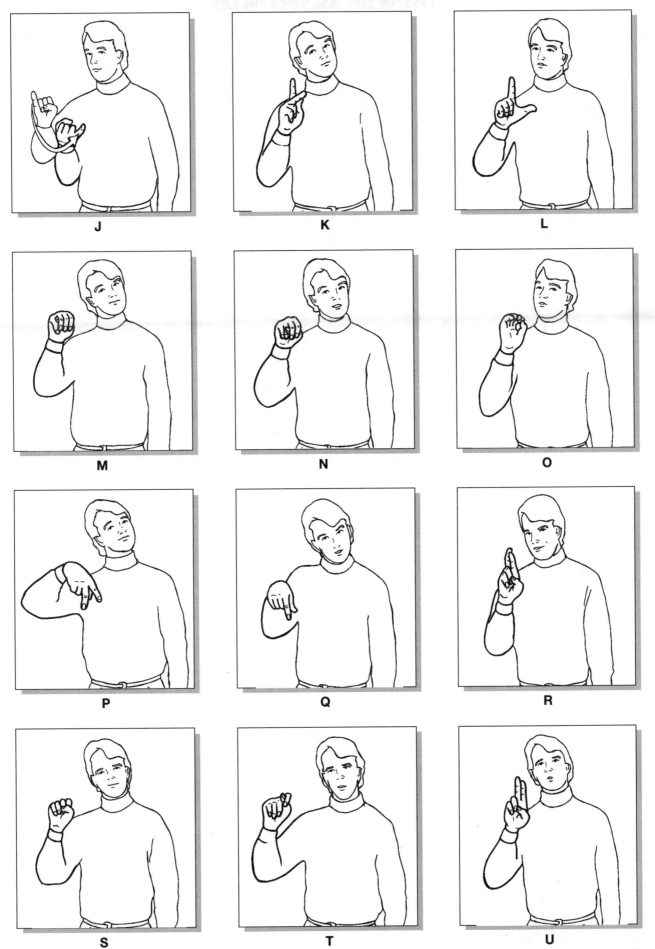

J

K

L

M

N

O

P

Q

R

S

T

U

SIGN ILLUSTRATIONS

V

W

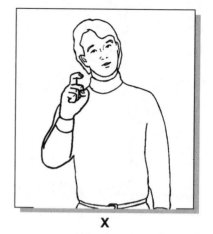

X

Y

Z

LESSON SEVEN: ASL VOCABULARY

BOOK

FINISH

FLOWER

GIVE

GOOD

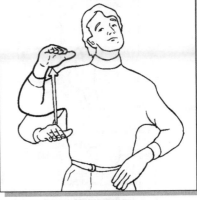

GROW-UP

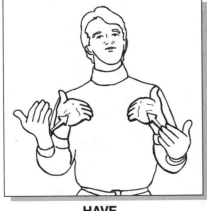

HAVE

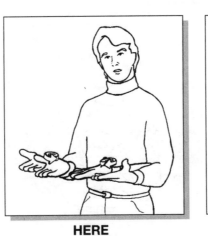

HERE

LATE

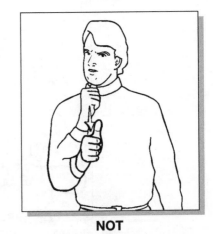

LEARN

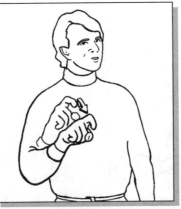

NEED

NOT

SIGN ILLUSTRATIONS

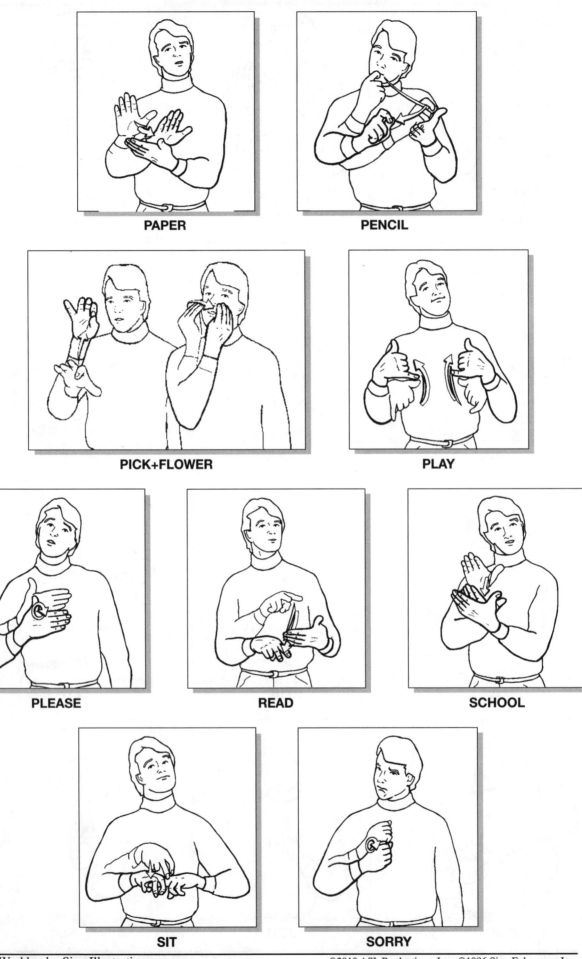

PAPER

PENCIL

PICK+FLOWER

PLAY

PLEASE

READ

SCHOOL

SIT

SORRY

SIGN ILLUSTRATIONS

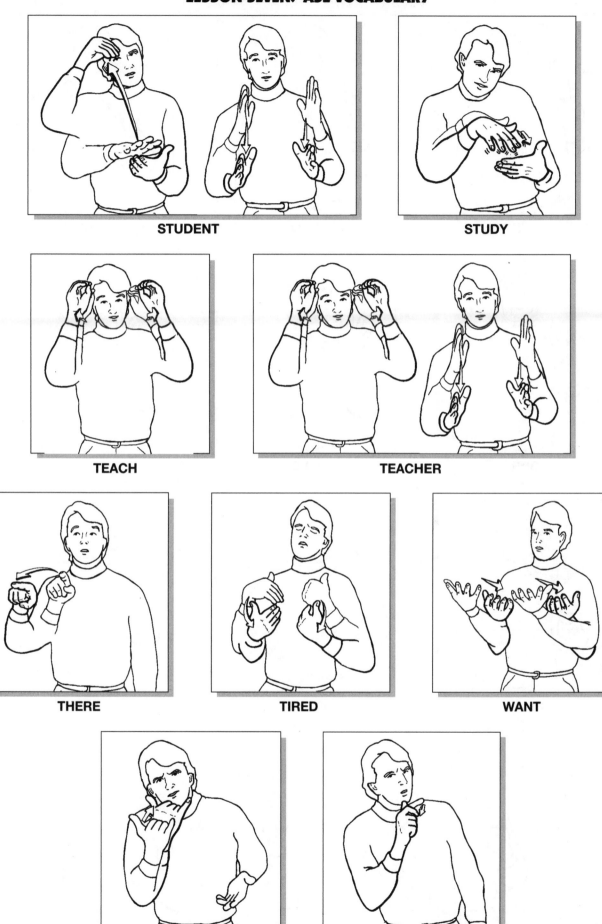

STUDENT

STUDY

TEACH

TEACHER

THERE

TIRED

WANT

WHAT-WRONG

WHO

SIGN ILLUSTRATIONS

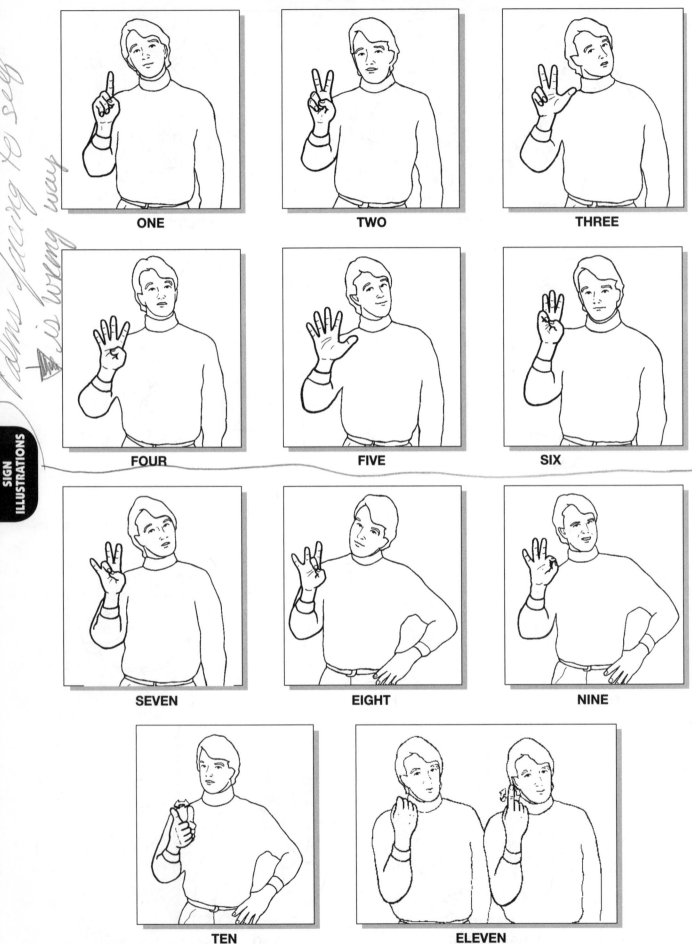

ONE

TWO

THREE

FOUR

FIVE

SIX

SEVEN

EIGHT

NINE

TEN

ELEVEN

Palms facing to self is wrong way

SIGN ILLUSTRATIONS

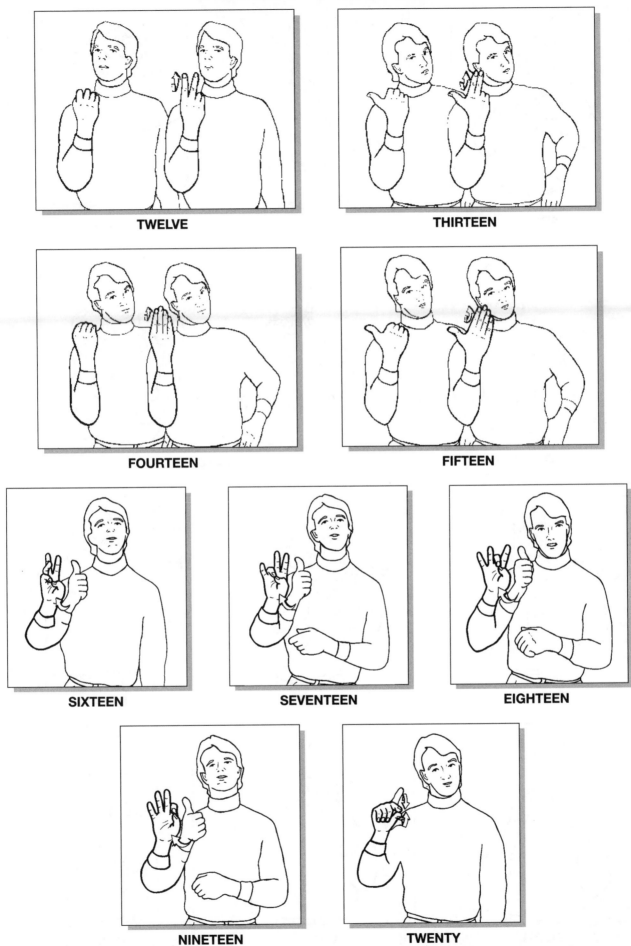

TWELVE

THIRTEEN

FOURTEEN

FIFTEEN

SIXTEEN

SEVENTEEN

EIGHTEEN

NINETEEN

TWENTY

LESSON EIGHT: ASL VOCABULARY

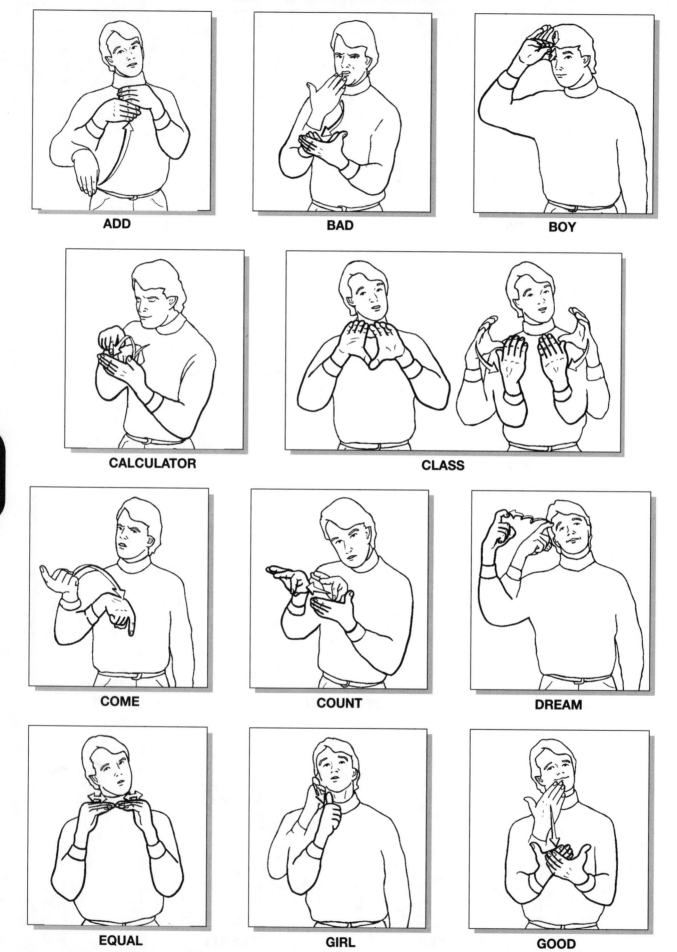

ADD

BAD

BOY

CALCULATOR

CLASS

COME

COUNT

DREAM

EQUAL

GIRL

GOOD

SIGN
ILLUSTRATIONS

LESSON EIGHT: ASL VOCABULARY

KNOW

MATH

MAYBE

MINUS/ NEGATIVE

NAME

PAY-ATTENTION

PLUS

PRINCIPAL

RIGHT/ CORRECT

ROOM

SLEEP

SIGN ILLUSTRATIONS

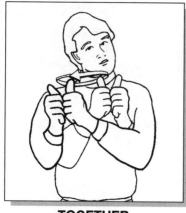

TOGETHER

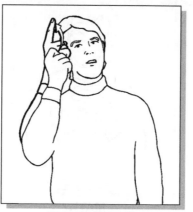

UNDERSTAND

WRONG/ INCORRECT

LESSON NINE: ASL VOCABULARY

ADDRESS

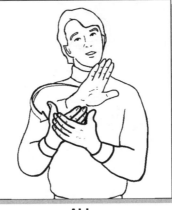

ALL

BALANCE

B-A-N-K

BIRTHDAY

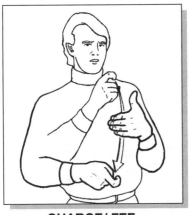

CHARGE/ FEE

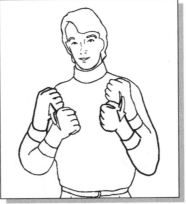

CHECK

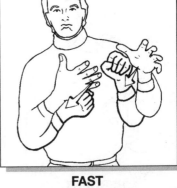

DEPOSIT

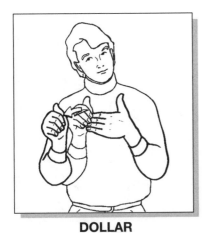

DOLLAR

DRIVE

FAST

LESSON NINE: ASL VOCABULARY

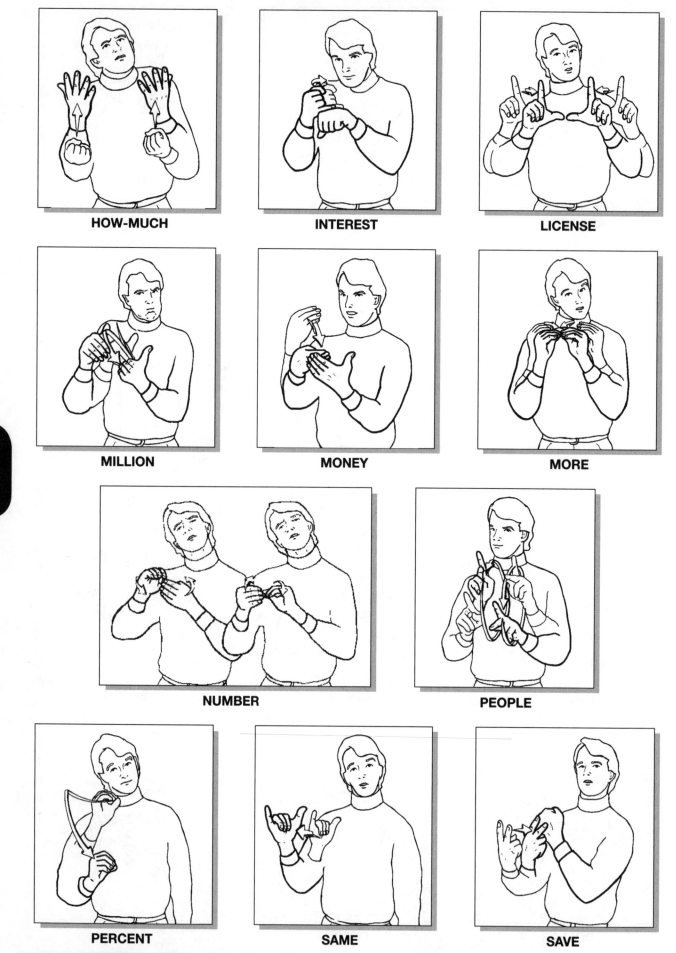

HOW-MUCH

INTEREST

LICENSE

MILLION

MONEY

MORE

NUMBER

PEOPLE

PERCENT

SAME

SAVE

SIGN ILLUSTRATIONS

LESSON NINE: ASL VOCABULARY

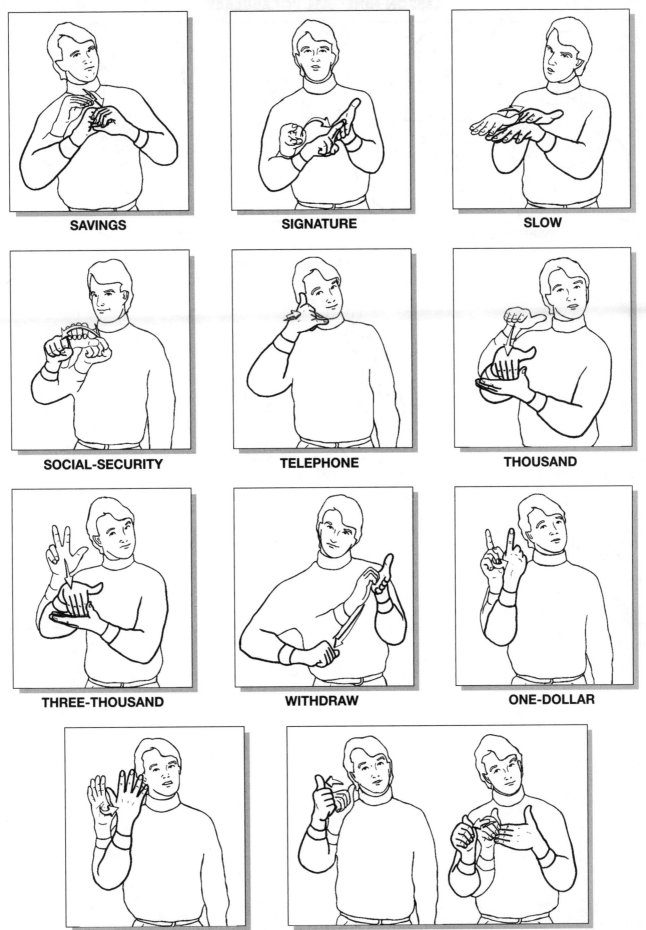

SAVINGS

SIGNATURE

SLOW

SOCIAL-SECURITY

TELEPHONE

THOUSAND

THREE-THOUSAND

WITHDRAW

ONE-DOLLAR

FIVE-DOLLAR

TEN+DOLLAR

SIGN ILLUSTRATIONS

TWENTY+DOLLAR

FIFTY+DOLLAR

100

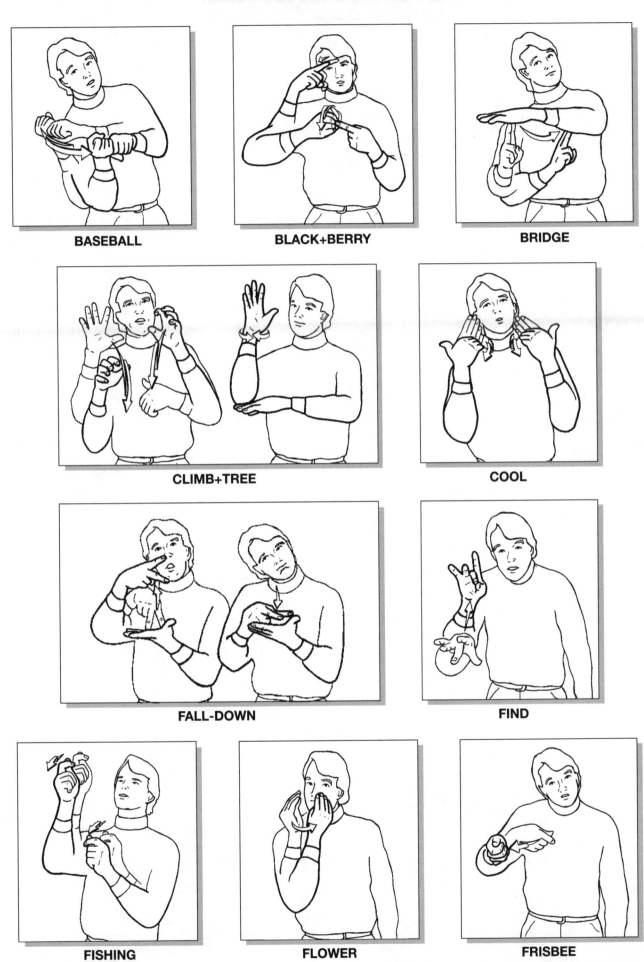

BASEBALL

BLACK+BERRY

BRIDGE

CLIMB+TREE

COOL

FALL-DOWN

FIND

FISHING

FLOWER

FRISBEE

SIGN ILLUSTRATIONS

GAME

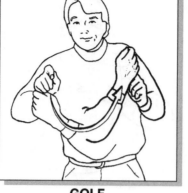

GOLF

GRASS

HOT

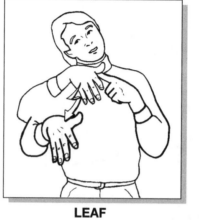

LEAF

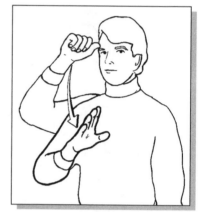

MAN

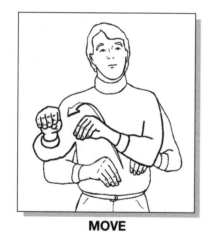

MOVE

PICNIC

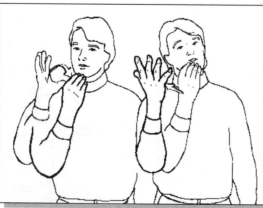

PRETTY/ BEAUTIFUL

PURSE/ BAG

LESSON ELEVEN: ASL VOCABULARY

RIVER

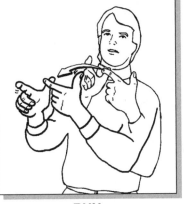

RUN

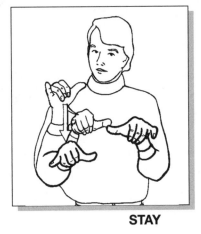

STAY

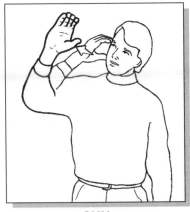

SUN

SUN+SHINE

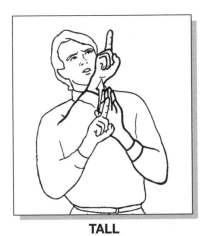

TALL

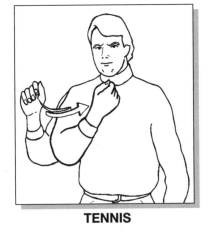

TENNIS

TREE

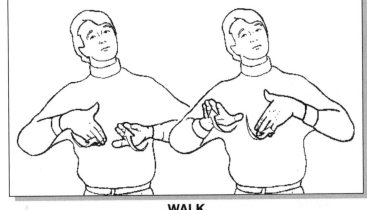

TREES/ FOREST

WALK

SIGN ILLUSTRATIONS

WATER

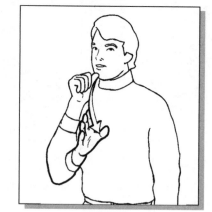

WOMAN

LESSON TWELVE: ASL VOCABULARY

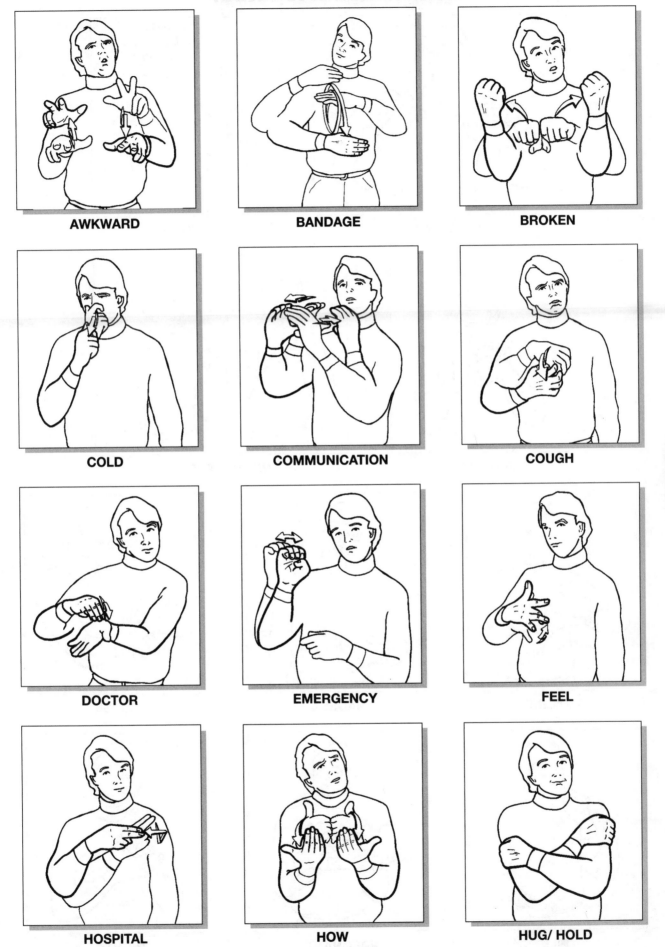

AWKWARD

BANDAGE

BROKEN

COLD

COMMUNICATION

COUGH

DOCTOR

EMERGENCY

FEEL

HOSPITAL

HOW

HUG/ HOLD

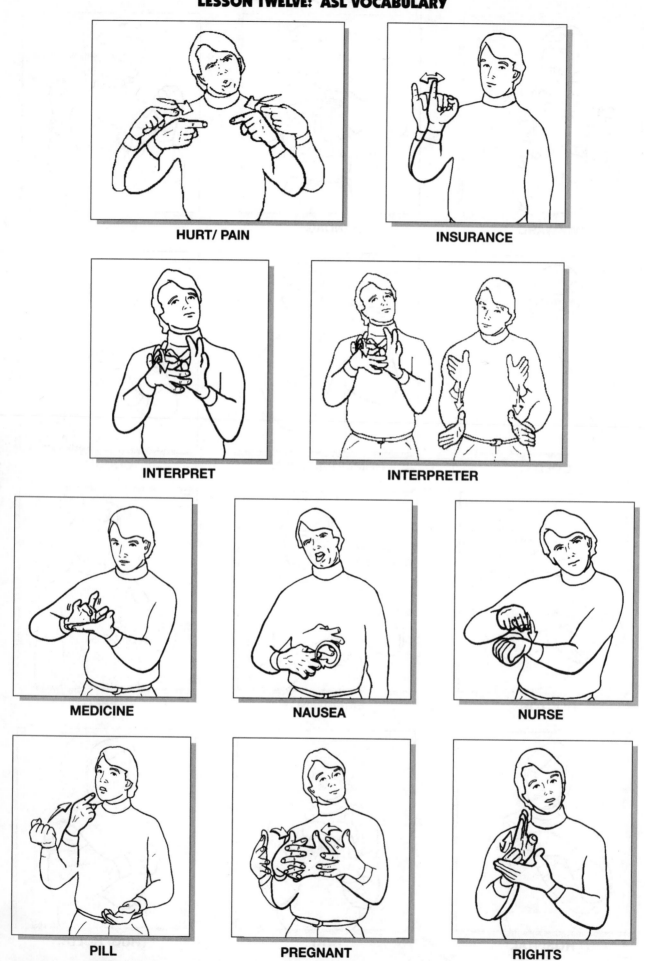

HURT/ PAIN

INSURANCE

INTERPRET

INTERPRETER

MEDICINE

NAUSEA

NURSE

PILL

PREGNANT

RIGHTS

ILLUSTRATIONS

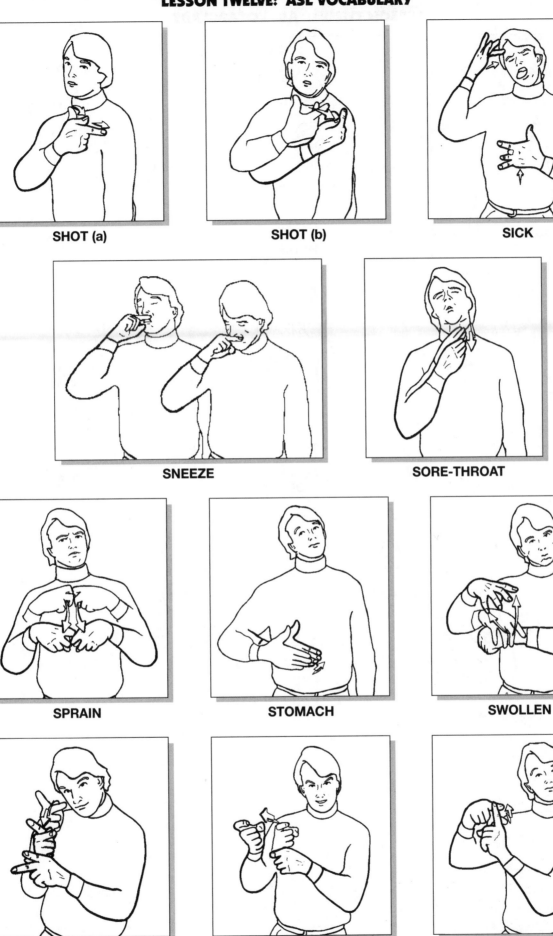

SHOT (a) SHOT (b) SICK

SNEEZE SORE-THROAT

SPRAIN STOMACH SWOLLEN

TAKE-CARE TEASE TEMPERATURE

SIGN ILLUSTRATIONS

LESSON TWELVE: ASL VOCABULARY

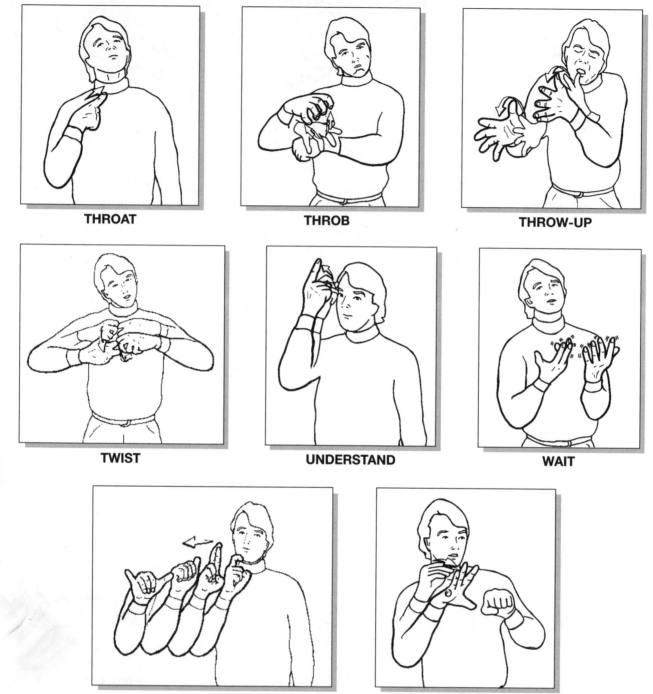

THROAT

THROB

THROW-UP

TWIST

UNDERSTAND

WAIT

X-R-A-Y

X-RAY

SIGN ILLUSTRATIONS

LESSON THIRTEEN: ASL VOCABULARY

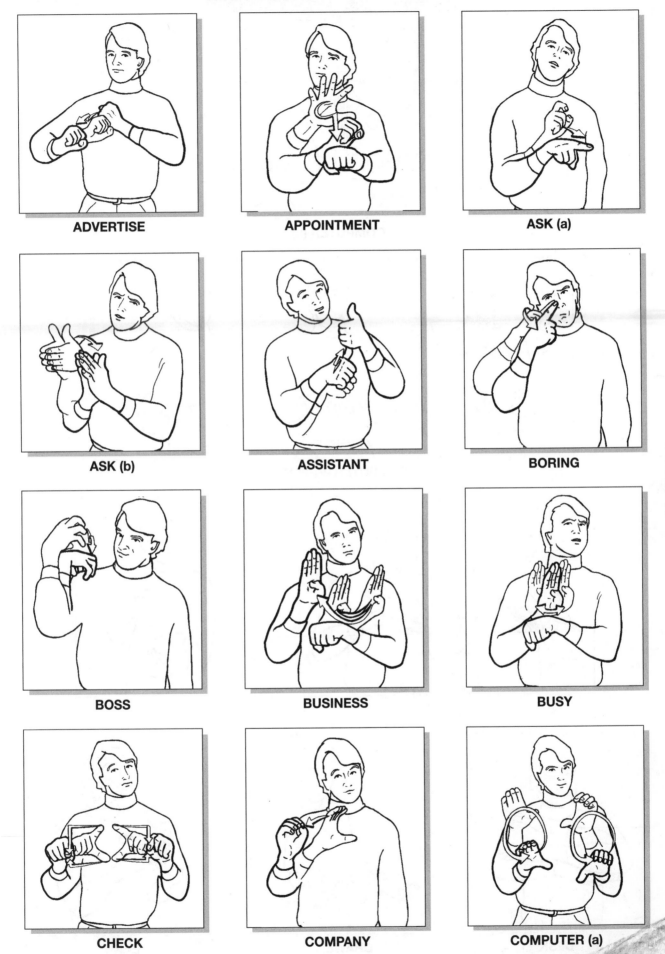

ADVERTISE

APPOINTMENT

ASK (a)

ASK (b)

ASSISTANT

BORING

BOSS

BUSINESS

BUSY

CHECK

COMPANY

COMPUTER (a)

SIGN ILLUSTRATIONS

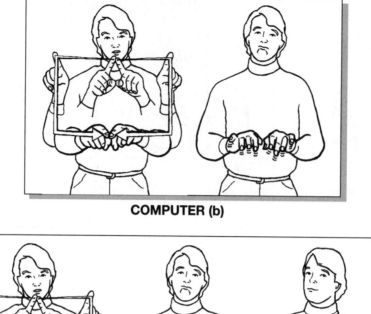

COMPUTER (b)

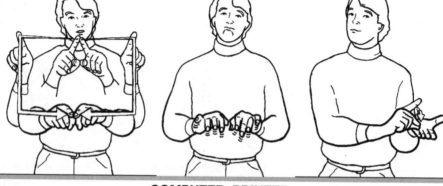

COMPUTER+PRINTER

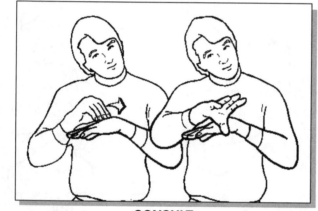

CONSULT

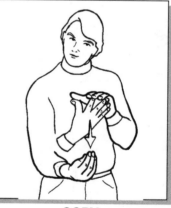

COPY

DESK

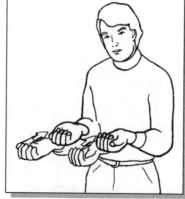

DRAWER

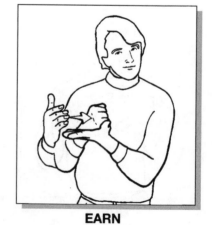

EARN

SIGN ILLUSTRATIONS

LESSON THIRTEEN: ASL VOCABULARY

ENVELOPE

EXPLAIN

FILE

FILES

FIRED

FIRST

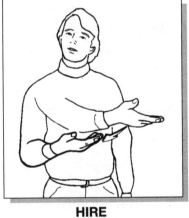

HIRE

IDEA

INTERVIEW

LAZY

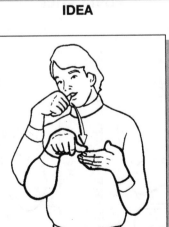

LETTER

MEETING

SIGN ILLUSTRATIONS

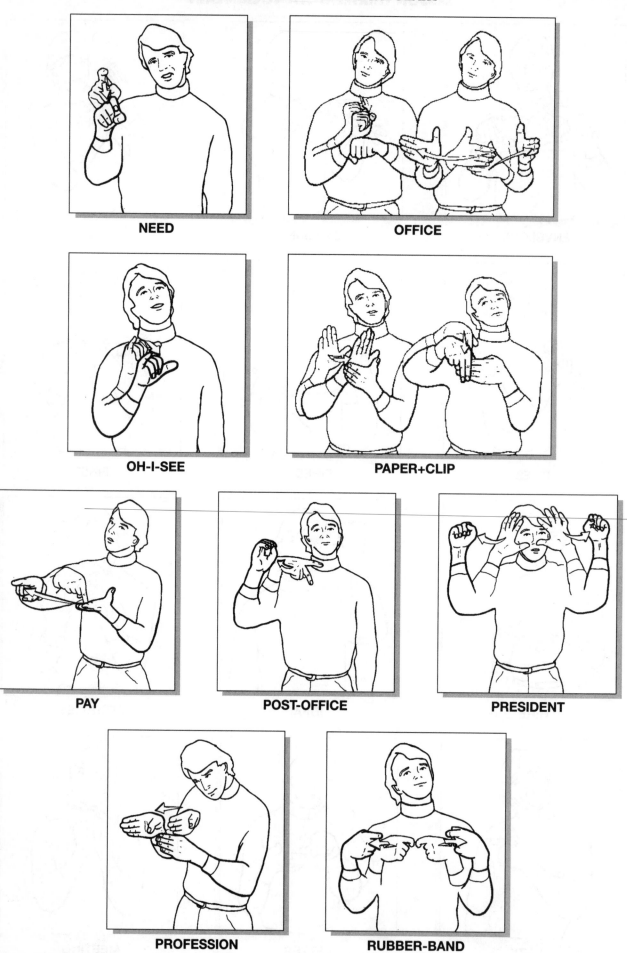

NEED

OFFICE

OH-I-SEE

PAPER+CLIP

PAY

POST-OFFICE

PRESIDENT

PROFESSION

RUBBER-BAND

Sign ILLUSTRATIONS

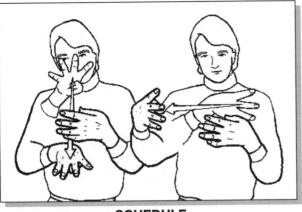

SCHEDULE

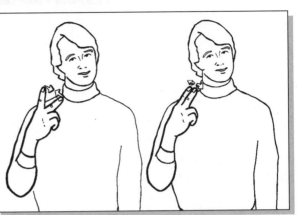

SCISSORS

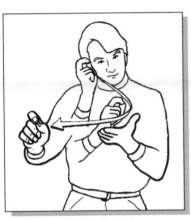

SECRETARY

SEND

SHELF

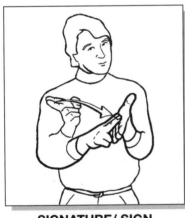

SIGNATURE/ SIGN

SKILL

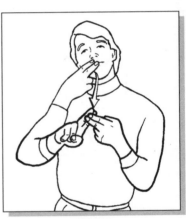

STAMP

STAPLE/ STAPLER

TAPE

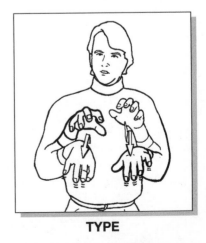

TYPE

Student Workbook: Sign Illustrations
Bravo ASL! Curriculum

S-43

SIGN ILLUSTRATIONS

TYPEWRITER

VICE-PRESIDENT

WORK

preposition

on
behind
in
under